Special gratitude to the following people:

Beulah Schoonover

Angus (Dave) Davenport

Michael and Jean Klepoch

Calvin Boerkoel

Lloyd and Doris Woodward

Vernon Wesch

Don Wixson

William Aitken

Dr. Leonard J. Boyer

Leonard Boyer, Jr.

B. J. and Sandry Smith

Ellan Ankle

I gratefully thank the following people for photographing their watch collections:

Adrian Blades	Kay Cook
Robert Churchill	Richard Roy
John Cargill	Howard Brumley
Ronald Bristol	Joseph Anthony
John MacDonald, Jr.	Al Asher

I dedicate this book to:

John Abbott	The Harry Lawrence Family
Dr. Albert Kallman	The Ted Lawrence Family
Sandra E. Criss	The Glenn Wells Family
Brian L. Criss	Melvin Dougherty, Jr.
Lee Criss	Rodney Stein
David Arlidge	Gordon Cook
Donald Thompson	Willis Lucro
Lowell Bristol	William Lucro
The Carson J. Montoney Family	Arthur Hale
The Late Joseph Montoney	Carol Criss and Rebecca
Donald Bass	Earl Schill
Greg Clark	Bob Hiltz
Lewis Berra	Glenn Sulkanen

Mary Baker

Dennis Peltennon and Family

Richard Rosenbaum

Richard Roy

The Late Ona Shaw

My Parents Richard and Marjorie Criss

Flora Arlidge

Richard and Arlene Bristol

Donald Hatfield

Ronda Craghead and Family

The Late Glenn Morrison

I gratefully thank the following people for their assistance:

Tammy Filer

John MacDonald, Sr.

Adrian Blades

Phyllis Bristol

John Dunn

Rodney Stein

I want to thank Ronald H. Bristol for his original inspiration and influence upon myself in writing and publishing this horological endeavor.

I dedicate this page to:

Robert Churchill

for his assistance in the final assembly of this book.

INDEX

INDEX

INTRODUCTION

This book will serve as a guide for gaining knowledge and information on all different makes of American pocket watches. It is a simple guide to a clear idea of what a pocket watch is worth. Pocket watches will be a fast growing hobby for Americans. They represent a piece of the history of our country from the time of the California Gold Rush. The railroads helped make Americans the greatest watchmakers in the world. At the turn of the century America was making some of the best watches that money could buy. The railroads demanded the best each company could produce. High jeweled movements offered the accuracy that the railroads demanded.

Both movements and cases were being produced with high standards of beauty and guarantee. Gold filled cases came in the guarantee of years of wear - 10 years, 15 years, 20 years, and the best, 25 years. Each year of the guarantee had a heavier layer of gold over the brass. Most cases were 14K gold and 10K on the lower priced watches. If the case was thin and soft, the disadvantage was that it could not be worn everyday. These were known as Sunday watches. These watches were sometimes given as gifts on anniversaries and graduations, as well as, presentation gifts and other special occasions. Sometimes it was a way of having gold around the house in case a person had to borrow money for an emergency.

The watch and the case in the old days were bought separately. The movements were sometimes low jeweled and cost less, but he or she might want a more expensive and beautiful case to show off to their friends. In the case of high jeweled railroad movements a strong case was used for wear and protection against shock. Today the quality of the case and the jewel content of the movement will determine the price of the watch, as well as wear, open face or hunting case, and type of metal.

IMPORTANT — Read the first 26 pages to get the full understanding and meaning of the guide book. Make sure you understand the watch book terms!

SPECIAL SUGGESTION

When one starts a nice collection of American pocket watches he will want to consider the following:

The collection should be stored in a dry and warm place. *Dampness is the number one danger.* Moisture will collect on the plates of watches and cause rust. The best way to store and protect your watch collection is in a *Foam Filled Attache Case.* Available from David Criss.

One should consider carrying a pocket watch. When buying a pair of slacks or trousers demand a watch pocket. When buying a suit be sure that the vest has two pockets. A watch chain can be worn across the front. A watch on one side and a coin or knife on the other side. This style of dress will be in fashion for years to come. For the lady, by all means, buy her a lady's 0s or 6s watch to hang from a neck chain.

FORWARD

This Pricing Guide is written for those people wanting to collect, buy, sell and trade watches. Every watch you acquire will have a personality of its own. Fascinating from the way it runs, to maybe who owned it, to who made it. At one time pocket watches were a status symbol. Everyone wanted to outdo the other person for beauty, quality, movement, and the metallic value of the case.

Solid gold was the tops in price and beauty. Sterling silver was next to gold. Sterling silver was scarce and underpriced for today's standards. One should add some of these to his collection.

Gold filled cases are the most popular of the watch collecting field. There were more made of this kind than any other metallic type. As the years of guarantee increased, the layers of gold plate became thicker. Brass was used too. Brass cases are very scarce, but when one finds one it will (most of the time) be priced cheaply. A hunting case will sell for around $50.00 to $70.00. You must add some to your collection.

Remember this is only a price guide; the pricing may or may not reflect the market price of a certain watch. This book can be a helpful source of information and may greatly influence the hobby itself.

After you get the feel of different makes of pocket watches, you may want to read more about the history of the Mfgr., and origin of the watch itself.

The first watch was made in Flanders about the turn of the sixteenth century.

PRICING GUIDE INFORMATION

1 — This book will be the first of a kind where a buying price will be established for watches. Other supplements will be added at a later time. All watches will be priced at the extremely fine grades.

2 — Cases with bad dents or worn very badly will be discounted by 50%. Fine to very fine are for watches running, no bad cracks in the dial, a nice case without bad wear or dents. Be very fair when buying or selling your watches. Beware of cheap or "HOT" buys in watches; most of the time there is something wrong with them.

3 — Movement screws that hold it in the case are important to the originality of the watch. Other screw marks make it not the original in the case. Discount these by 25%. After the price from the guide is established say like $130.00 for a hunting case watch and the screws are not matching in place, then take off 25% or the price will be $98.00.

4 — Watches with fancy dials add 20%. They can have a minimum of cracks and be worth 10% more.

5 — Solid gold cases like 10K and 14K have been common in the past, but are becoming hard to find. 18K is scarce and should be twice the price of the 14K. The 22K case is very rare today. They should be priced twice that of the 18K case. Mint watches are rare and should command top prices. If they have a lot of engraving on them add 50% more. Plain cases should not be overlooked, they can be engraved with animals, boats, scenes, or your own initials. These can be bought very reasonably in today's market.

DAMASKEENING ON THE WATCH PLATES

As the watch industry began to advance in the late 70's and early 80's, each watch company tried to produce the best. Prices seemed not to enter into the picture.

Some went as far as matching the beauty of the movement to the beauty of the dial and case. For example, multi-colored case, multi-colored dial, and multi-colored movement.

Some of the finest watches came from this period of time, 1880 to 1900.

Movements were not only precision made, but they had to have beautiful color damasking swirled into the metal. Seth Thomas, Rockford, Waltham, Ill., and many other companies competed for the field of beauty. Again after 1900 prices squeezed a lot of the companies out of the business. They could no longer put this extra special art into movements. When you come across these kinds of beautifully damasked movements you should add them to your collection.

SPECIAL INFORMATION ON THE MOVEMENTS

Jewel Settings

Jewel settings are made of brass and gold. Hampden Watch Co. tried to press them into the plate. This proved to be inefficient because of the expansion of the steel from the heat and cold. Consequently the jewels would crack and the watch would stop running. The only way was using brass and gold. The jewels could be set and held by screws. Gold was used in the better and more expensive models. Gold jewel settings are found in the high priced watches of their day. So look for these and maybe you will find these watches priced very reasonably.

Gears

Gears in watches were also made of brass and gold. Brass being more common. Gold was used in the more expensive watches. Like gold settings, the gears would not become magnetic and would run more accurately. They also would not be affected by heat and cold. In the high priced watch you had the whole gear train in gold, starting from the center gear through the fourth gear. The fourth gear was the second hand, made the cost of the watch higher. Some had only the center gear in gold; these would cost $10.00 to $20.00 less.

Look for the gear train in the watch you buy. It may only be a 15 jewel or a 17 jewel watch, but at the time it was made, it could have cost double the price of a regular watch.

TYPES OF CASES

Box
: Regular type Hunting case, but with a box type hinge at the top and bottom.
Made in both open face and Hunting and in all size of cases. **Rare**

Hunting
: A cover over the crystal, popular Sunday watch. **Scarce**

Display
: Used in jewelry stores to see movements.

Open Face
: Common type case for everyday use. **Common**

Convertible
: Convert into open face or Hunting. **Rare**

Multi-color
: Up to 5 colors of gold laid on gold filled or solid gold. **Scarce**

Demi-Hunting
: Common name for half Hunter. Most of these cases were popular in England and Scotland. Waltham made some of these, but they are scarce. They were made so that a person could see the time without opening the front cover. This would keep your lock on the front cover from wearing out faster. **Semi-scarce**

Clam Shell
: Used mostly on 6s ladies' watches. Sometimes on men's open face watches. About 20 blunt triangle shaped edges protruding about the center frame of watch. **Scarce**

Rope Type
: Looks like the edge of a rope, encircling the edge of the watch. Used in both open face and Hunting watches. **Scarce**

Pear Shape
: Most often found in open face 12s watches.

5 Sided
: More commonly used in 12 size open face watches.

6 Sided
: More commonly used in 12 size open face watches. **Common**

"THE BEST WINNERS OF 1975"

14K and 18K Hunting Cases, 16s and 18s
Up and Down Indicators
24J and 25J watches
Repeaters — Swiss and English type
Multi-Color watches
Box Cases

"I PREDICT THE FOLLOWING FOR 1976-77"
TO BE THE BEST WINNERS

Fancy Dials Os, Gs, 8s, 12s, 16s, 18s, and 22s
23J watches and odd jewels
14K and 18K watches in OF or hunting
Silver case watches, silver will be higher
Keywinds, the antiques of watch collecting
Multi-color watches, this art is lost
Repeaters, made today in Switzerland would cost $6,000 to
    $10,000
18s, 15J, and 17J of common watches
12s and 16s watches for everyday use

Like the hobby of collecting coins, some makes of watches are worth more than other makes. This guide will give you an idea of which makes are more scarce. We will note these makes as starting from rare to common, the number of jewels and the special models each company made will be noted also. This is a very important point to consider if you are collecting or selling. The following will be for movement rating.

GRADING OF CASE AND MOVEMENT

CASE
Mint	In the box.
Brilliant Unc.	No wear, but been handled.
Extremely Fine,	Slight wear, one dent and dial hairline.
Very Fine	Even wear, slight defect.
Fine	Even wear, minor dents and some defects.
Good	Gold worn, minor dents
Poor	Gold worn thru brass, broken or many dents.

MOVEMENTS
Mint	Never been repaired, running, no marks or scratches.
E.F.	Been repaired, but running good and has a perfect balance.
Fine	Movement has scratches and not been repaired well.
Very Good	Not running, but all parts are there.
Poor	Not running, parts missing.

GRADING FOR WATCHES

Grading for watches in this guide is for E.F. Don't over grade! Extra fine watches should look like new, but may have a dent or slight wear on the case — very slight.

MOVEMENT RATING

Rare	Rare
Scarce	7-15 jewel Hamiltons
Semi-scarce	Any 24J or more watches
Very desirable	Repeating watches
Common	Very early serial numbers
	Transition models
	Up and down indicators

Common and or not so common
7-15 or 17 jewels are the most common type. Special names and models on movements are not so common. A 15J Hamilton and 16J Elgin are scarce.

Name	Model Numbers of Movements	
John Hancock	Hamilton	South Bend
Abe Lincoln	940	431
Wm. McKinley	992	429
Railroad	992B	419
BunnJ	950	207
Bunn Special	996	
Maiden Lane	944	
Riverside Maximum		
etc., etc., etc.		
Sangamo		
Veritas		
Father Time		
Studebaker		
Vanguard		
B. W. Raymond	Charles Fargo	
Mat Laflin	Francis Ruby	
J. T. Ryerson	Gail Borden	
H. H. Taylor	Dexter St.	
H. L. Culver	W. H. Perry	
J. V. Farwell		

DIALS

The following are names of the dials that are scarce and hard to find without cracks or hairlines. This is what makes a scarce watch scarce. The dials are hard to replace most of the time. If you had a Studebaker by South Bend with a bad dial, the price may be worth $150.00, but with a bad dial the price will be discounted by 25 percent. So when buying you must keep these dials in mind as to where or how you can replace them.

Very Scarce	Common to Scarce
Howard	South Bend
Aurora	Burlington
Ball	Trenton
Cheshire	U.S. Watch Co., Waltham
Columbus	Edgemere
Keystone	Equity
Ingersoll, Trenton	Dueber-Hampden
Lancaster	Elgin
New England	Hamilton
Peoria	Illinois
Rockford	N.Y. Standard
Seth Thomas	Waltham
	Washington, Ill.

HANDLING OF THE WATCH

For open face watches you must not pull hard on the stem and crown. Sometimes they are dirty and frozen and will need cleaning. Stems and crowns today are hard to find and without them the case is worthless. On some makes by screwing off the crystal and bezel you will see a lever at two o'clock. This lever will come out with the pull of your finger nail. This will in turn free the hands and then you can go ahead and turn the hands with the crown and stem.

Hunting Cases

DON'T SNAP THE FRONT COVER. This is 99 percent of the problem with amateurs. The cover is opened with the push of the crown and closed with the push of the crown. The cover catch is on the inside rim and if it is snapped enough times it will wear away the gold or silver and will need repair. Never push in the center of the cover when closing. It will break the crystal or bend the cover in the middle.

Swing Out Movements

Some open face watches swing out from the front. By screwing off the crystal you will see a groove at 6 o'clock. First pull out the stem. Be careful that you don't pull too hard or it will come out all together. It is best to turn it and then with your thumb nail flip it up towards you. DON'T FORCE IT. You may break the stem off. To loosen the stem, dunk it into a cup of acetone to free the dirt and grease that may hold it from coming out.

Snap Off Backs

On some watch cases, the back cover snaps on and off. Look for a small crack on the back at 2 o'clock. Use a small pocket knife and pry away from yourself. It should snap right off. If there is no crack, it will screw off. DON'T PRY, unless you first try to screw it off.

POSITION OF WATCHES

The position of the watch is a term used to indicate how accurate it can run to the position it is in. Like 3 position watch means running accurate in a vertical, horizontal, and maybe between these positions. 5 positions watch comes under the railroad grade of watch. The more the positions the more accurate the watch. This is why they cost so much more than everyday watches. High position watches say like 7 or more are rare, so look for one of these for your collection.

SPECIAL TYPE MOVEMENTS

Up and Down Indicators

These watches were made for the railroad; they had a little dial and hand at the 12 o'clock position. This indicated the number of hours that were left on the mainspring. This would prevent one from overwinding the mainspring.

Transition Models

A type of watch that was converted from a keywind to a stem wind. It will have a place on the mainspring barrel to wind with a key.

60 Hour Bunn

Mainsprings are capable of running for 60 hours; scarce, but sells for about the same as a regular Bunn.

Repeating Watch

A repeating watch is one in which the time can be heard in the dark of night by pushing a slide lever on the side of the watch; it would chime off the time.

1/4 hour	It will chime the hours and quarter hours
5 minutes	It will chime the hours, quarter hours
Minute	It will chime the hours, quarter hours and the minutes after the quarter hours

Convertible

A type of movement made by the Elgin Co. It worked like a TRANSMISSION. When you pulled out the stem to set the hands this gear would engage into the center gear and the hands would then turn for setting the time. Odd, but this movement is very scarce.

THE HISTORY OF EDWARD HOWARD
AND THE HOWARD WATCH

The American watch, like practically every other great achievement of American inventors, was wrought out under discouragements that would have appalled ordinary men.

While Morse was struggling against the sickening disappointments of the telegraph, and Goodyear was undergoing privations in his search for the secret of curing India rubber, Edward Howard, with the assistance of capital furnished by friends, was struggling with the creation of the watch industry.

Edward Howard was apprenticed in 1829 to Aaron Willard, Jr., son of Aaron Willard, who was the youngest of three brothers, born in Grafton, Mass.

The Willards were noted for their fine clock work. Simon, the oldest, settled in Roxbury in 1771 at the "Sign of the Clock." He made his first clock at the age of 13, and was the most ingenious of all the Willards. He made Turret Clocks for Boston, Philadelphia, New York and the University of Virginia. While in Virginia he became acquainted with Jefferson and Madison, with whom he corresponded for years. He never considered profit, the quality of work being everything. His clocks, great and small, are just as good, after the lapse of a century, as when they left his hands.

Aaron Willard, Jr. learned the trade from his father, and to him Edward Howard was apprenticed in 1829. Young Howard was a mechanical genius.

It was natural that he should consort with the best watchmakers he could find. Watchmaking fascinated him. He studied it; saw its weaknesses, and dreamed of overcoming them and of revolutionizing the watch industry of the world.

He further says: "I know from experience that there was no proper system employed in making watches. The work was all done by hand. Now handwork is superior in many of the arts because it allows variation according to the individuality of the worker.

"But in the exquisitely fine wheels and screws and pinions that make up the parts of a watch, the less variation the better."

This idea of automatic machines was daring and revolutionary enough in all conscience. Yet he says of it simply; "The development of the plan was the result of long thinking;" and further; "I came in for much ridicule from those to whom I confided it. They laughingly said, and I thought with some reason, that one of my machines if I ever got it running, would be a greater marvel than the finest watch that ever was made".

Howard went into business for himself in 1840, risking all that he possessed and all that he could command from his friends who believed in him. He determined to establish systematic watchmaking and to invent labor-saving machinery for producing perfect interchangeable parts.

His first step was to build a factory in Roxbury, Mass. The first watch factory in the new world.

Writing of this period he says: "It is almost needless to say that we met with many obstacles. We were told by importers and dealers in watches that we would never be able to carry out our plans and that our project would be an utter failure. Some of our friends even told us we were crazy to attempt such an undertaking.

"But we were Americans and had a sufficient quantity of the proverbial grit, and at least believed in ourselves even if others did not have so much faith.

"We could not import and use foreign help, unacquainted with our methods and tools. So we had to instruct our men from the beginning. There were many times when we felt that the predictions of the importers would prove true, but perseverance conquered.

"The financial problem was a hard matter to solve, as the unbelief in our process was universal. Frequently it was difficult to raise the money needed to get materials or pay our workmen. We struggled along for six years before the tide turned.

"Without the financial assistance of good friends in Boston, watchmaking would probably not have existed at the present time as an organized industry in the United States. This may seem to be a sweeping statement, but no one can conceive the trials we endured. We hear about going through purgatory, but that must be a pleasure compared with what we experienced at that time.

"We were trying to establish under one roof an industry embracing a dozen distant trades. Such a thing had never been done before and we were still further handicapped in our undertaking by having inexperienced assistants. We had to teach others. Our progress was slow and expensive and there was much bad work that we had to throw away.

"Our first watch was made to run for eight days, but was discarded because the mainspring was too long and cumbersome.

"We did not know how to make a jewel or a dial or to do proper watch gilding or to produce a mirror finish on steel. We had to study and work over these operations until after many attempts, one at last would be successful.

"We had to invent all the tools to make the different parts. After being designed or invented they had to be made in the factory by our own machinists in order to have them perfect and durable. Attempts were made to have them made outside, but it was impossible to get them constructed carefully and of the exact and uniform sizes needed.

"It was nearly three years before the establishment had fairly and fully started in the business of making watches, and then we found that we needed ten times as much room so we set about building a very much larger factory at Waltham, Mass.

"The expenses of this new factory were greater than was anticipated. The constant experimenting, the cost of working models, the spoiled materials, rejected work, the building of new machines and the comparatively small marketable output, a thousand discouragements and the antagonism of the entire watch and jewelry trade finally brought matters to a crisis and Howard saw ruin staring him in the face. Some of his associates complained that he was too scrupulous about the perfection of the watches that left his hands."

He says on this point: "Friends turned from me saying I was not practical. Workmen who left me or were discharged complained that I was exacting and expected the impossible because I would not tolerate a botch of any kind. I would rather break a watch movement than have it go out imperfect. My standard for every watch that bore my name was that it be fit to present to the President of the United States. They had me quite humbled and ashamed with the thought that I was not fair to those interested. But I could not bring myself to do otherwise."

Now comes the most important work that Edward Howard accomplished in the direction of timekeeping accuracy.

We have noted his complaint of the variation of individual parts made by hand and learned how he overcame the difficulty.

Next we find him making a curious discovery, viz; "Every watch has its individuality. Pick out and put together two sets of absolutely perfect individual parts made by machinery that does not vary one twenty-thousandth of an inch, run them under exactly the same conditions and each watch will vary slightly from the other and from the standard."

He had gotten away from individuality in the parts only to meet it again in the assembly movement, and discovery was the beginning of the Howard constructive adjustment.

It takes months to adjust a Howard watch not withstanding the fact that it's a better timekeeper than many a high grade watch when it is first put together. The Howard requirements are higher.

It is run and timed for a period on its face, on its back, in different positions. Then in an over intense heat, then in a refrigerator under extreme cold, accurate record being kept of its performance from day to day.

When it varies it goes into the hands of an expert who overhauls it until he finds the cause of the variation, corrects it — then the watch starts on its test performance all over again.

The result is that the Howard adjustment when completed is good for fifty years (barring accident or violence). It will stand more jolt and jar than any other watch, being adjusted to vibration as well as change of temperature.

Howard thought more of his scientific adjustments than anything else he accomplished. He left minute instructions and provisions for its continuance along with certain data that he would never divulge during his lifetime nor trust even with his patent authorities, though it is likely the matters were not in their nature subject to patent right protection.

Previous to 1853 the American markets were controlled by Swiss and English makers and there was much prejudice against Howard's products.

Howard writes in 1850: "Americans have never been free from a snobbishness that loves to display a foreign trademark. Just as the foot man is more lordly than his master, so the tradesman is more snobbish than his customer .

"Of course, men who were looking at the financial side could not feel as I did about my watch. They could not understand that the watch was the end I sought, that I would give everything I possessed, even life itself, to see all work out as I had planned."

This was the temper of Therman as attested by all who knew him. It was currently believed at the time that Howard was the model for the character of Owen Warland in Nathaniel Hawthorne's short story the **"Artist of the Beautiful."**

Howard was a workman of astonishing dexterity and the highest ideals. His venture created a great deal of stir, because of its apparent impracticability, and Hawthorne living in Concord at the time, could not have failed to hear a great deal of it. The story was published in June, 1844, only a year or so after the first Howard watch was completed.

The Howard factory failed in 1857. The plant, tools and machinery were taken over by men in Waltham and became the nucleus of the great industry there, and incidentally the parent of watch factories in other parts of the country.

Howard's characteristic comment on this state of affairs was this: "I had to begin at the bottom and make all tools anew. I returned to my old factory at Roxbury, founded a new company with the understanding that I was to have my say about the quality of watches that bore the Howard name."

How he succeeded is a matter of history. The output was limited by Howard, but the watch was a priced possession. Men paid $500.00 for them in the early sixties.

A prominent citizen of Philadelphia (a retired businessman) wrote the Howard factory recently that he had personally carried a Howard watch for fifty years and that its variation today is not more than one second in twenty-four hours, or one second in eighty-six thousand.

Howard had perfected his marvelous automatic machinery for making the delicate watch parts so that of a thousand pieces, one would be exactly like the other.

Three thousand two hundred patents granted by the Patent Office in Washington in the field of watch and clock invention are directly or indirectly due to his initiative.

He had made the first practical application of the stem winding mechanism designed in a crude form by a London watchmaker in 1750.

But in spite of the ban on Howard by importers and retail jewelers, he was instrumental establishing through the Howard watch the reputation of American-made watches the world over as the best.

In 1866, American watches were extensively introduced in London. The English watch industry declined. English makers came here and bought American watch machinery, but could do little with it. Howard forced foreign makers to buy American machinery and foreign watches are made on American machines today.

There is a record for you. The half-baked Roxbury boy with his idea—the scoff and butt of his companions—yet he broke the back of a world industry and brought the richest guilds in Europe to Massachusetts begging for his machinery that they might continue their trade. And yet there are American jewelers who offer foreign watches as a superior article.

Years later, the Howard Factory was again removed to the Waltham—the scene of its early failures—where it is now established as a splendid enterprise and a monument to a man who believed in himself; who countenanced no shame in his work and who lived to make the finest watches in the world.

THE END

A HISTORY OF THE WALTHAM WATCH COMPANY
IN ITS EARLY YEARS

To trace the early years of the Waltham Watch Co. it is necessary to go back to the year 1850 in Roxbury, Massachusetts at 34 Water Street. In September of that year, we find a company by the name of Howard, Davis and Dennison located at that address. It is not surprising, when you consider the name of the company, that the principal officers were: Edward Howard; David P. Davis; and Aaron L. Dennison. Howard, Davis and Dennison had joined together in the time honored enterprise of watchmaking.

Mr. Howard was apprenticed in 1829 to Aaron Willard, Jr. Being a mechanical genius, Howard was fascinated by watchmaking. Being associated with the watchmakers and clockmakers of the period, he was able to see the shortcomings of the watch industry of the day. The main drawback was the practice of making watches by hand. Howard dreamed of producing watches faster by automatic machines. Edward Howard was more than a dreamer—he was a doer, as we shall see.

In 1842, Howard formed a partnership with David Davis to manufacturer clocks and balance scales. The firm made banjo clocks in the Willard Style.

In 1830, Aaron L. Dennison was serving his apprenticeship in Brunswick, N.H. After finishing his apprenticeship, he moved to Boston, where he became employed by Jones, Low, and Ball. Like Howard, Dennison was very interested in machine production of watches. Then he met Howard!

Howard showed great interest in Dennison's ideas, but neither had enough capital to start a factory. This problem was solved by Samuel Curtis, who provided the necessary financing. By the summer of 1850 a "model" watch was completed. This first watch was made similar to the English style.

By January of 1851, their factory building was completed. During this year they took the name American Horologe Company. The first machine made watches were completed by late 1852.

The name American Horologe Company only lasted about six months. The new name was Warren Manufacturing Company, named after the famed revolutionary war hero, who had lived in the area.

The first 17 watches were not placed on the market. They were given to members of the company. The first market watches appeared in 1853, and were numbered 18 - 120. They were marked "Warren". Also, in 1853 the company name was again changed. This time to Boston Watch Company.

The next 800 watches were marked "Samuel Curtis" and a few were marked "Fellows & Schell". (Fellows & Schell or Shell was an exclusive dealership in New York City that had assisted them in financial problems.)

On October 5, 1854 they moved into a new building in Waltham. The movements made in this new building started with #1001. Movements from 1001 - 5,000 were marked Dennison, Howard and Davis; C.T. Parket: and P.S. Bartlett.

In 1857, the Boston Watch Co. failed and was sold at Sheriff's auction. It was purchased by Royal E. Robbins. The new company was organized as Tracy, Baker & Co. There were apparently some disagreements in the leadership of the company and in May of 1857 the company was reorganized as Appleton, Tracy & Co. The first movements were marked Appleton, Tracy & Co. and started with #5,001. These, like previous models, were made with unmarked dials. The first marked dials occurred around #6500 and were marked Appleton, Tracy & Co.

The principal officers of the Appleton, Tracy & Co. were: H. Adams, President; James W. Appleton, Partner; Royal E. Robbins, Partner; A.L. Dennison, Partner; and Daniel Appleton, Partner. They made their first watch in the fall of 1857 (#5,001 - 14,000). 598 chronometers were made in December of 1858. The C.T. Parker model was introduced in 1857, and the P.S. Bartlett model in January of 1858.

The 1857-1859 period was a time of economic depression in America. Appleton, Tracy & Co. was having a very hard time. On January 1, 1859 they merged with the Waltham Improvement Company.

The Waltham Improvement Co. had been established in 1852 to promote and establish a factory at Waltham. 40 percent of the stock was held by the Boston Watch Co.—but now the two were merged into the American Watch Company.

Among the leadership of the American Watch Co. were people who would be important to the company in later years. Some of these names were: Charles V. Woerd; Charles W. Fogg; and William Ellery. Among the established members of the company there was A.L. Dennison; R.E. Robbins and E. Tracy.

The Civil War was a time of extreme turbulance in America. It was however, a period of prosperity for the American Watch Company, due to the labors of R.E. Robbins. Mr. Robbins saw the potential of an economically priced watch of high quality. He was successful in marketing this watch. His customers were the soldiers of the Civil War. From this time forward the American Watch Company was on a firm financial footing.

In 1861, the R.E. Robbins model was established, followed by the William Ellery Model in 1863. By 1877, the first chronograph was available. This in turn was followed in 1883 by the first split second hand.

In 1862, the Nashua Watch Company was purchased for $23,000. About 1,000 movements were included in this purchase.

About 1862, a number of the company leaders left to become employed by the National Watch Company of Chicago. The National Watch Co., of course, was later known as the Elgin Watch Company

In 1885, the company name was again changed to: **THE AMERICAN WALTHAM WATCH COMPANY.**

Among the success stories in American free enterprises, the Waltham Watch Company success must be rated high. By 1953 there had been well over 33,000,000 Waltham watches produced. 33,000,000 watches were not produced without trial, and many many problems, but the problems only served as a challenge to a group of men that had a good idea and knew it! What was more important, they believed in their ideas and in themselves enough to make the sacrifices that were necessary to attain success. They had learned through the course of their own lives that success is only one step beyond failure. If they had stopped at the difficult times, they would have indeed failed, but they continued trying, never admitting failure. Our forefathers were strong willed and determined people and we have today what is a very high standard of living because of their spirit of sacrifice—the strength and spirit of sacrifice is alive today!

WATCH CASE HISTORY, CASE MANUFACTURING AND TESTING PROCEDURES

The U.S. was the only country in the world by 1900 that could produce a well made gold filled case that could be sold cheaply to the public.

Europeans tried for many years, but their gold filled cases would only wear a few years before the case would show brass.

The lower priced European watches were made of the following materials: black gun metal, brass case, and silver. For beauty European watches were made in gold, but were very costly.

This is where the great American enterprise took the lead in watch case manufacturing throughout the world.

"Case Manufacturing"

The process used in gold filled was simple in content. As one would coin a phrase: "Why didn't I think of that?"

Step 1: They used a rectangular sheet of brass or composition metal soldered between two sheets of gold. Then these sheets were rolled to the desired thickness of the size required. The thickness of the gold would result in the number of years of wear as follows: 5 years; 10 years; 15 years; 20 years; 25 years; and 25 extra. Most often 14K gold was used, but frequently, only 10K was used in railroad watch cases.

After the rolling process they stamped out the desired diameters larger than the actual watch. Then they stamped, in cup shape, the form to the actual size of the watch cover desired.

After that the edges were rolled over to form the catch. If there was any engraving on the cover it was done at the same time as the preceding process.

The next process was the manufacture of the rim of the watch case. A band of gold filled was made from strips of rolled gold, then made round and soldered at the top, similar to a gold wedding band, etc.

This was fitted into a die which was shaped to the size desired for the curves of a watch case rim. Then they would fit a band of gold into this die, and using a roller or wheel shaped disk, which had a shaft connected thru the center of this roller which would spin around inside of the die and thus shape the rim. There could be many rollers connected to the shaft making many rollers connected to the shaft making many case rims at the same time. The size of the inside of the case conforming to the size of the watch, which was excess metal, was turned on a lathe to conform to the watch movement size.

A pendent bow which held the crown and stem was soldered to the desired point of the watch case and rim in which, of course, a hole had been drilled previously. A similar tube of gold was then soldered to the desired cover placement. The same process was also done to the cover. Then they placed these to the case rim and with a small wire connected them to the rim joints.

In order to clearly understand the preceding procedures, take an old hunting watch case and go through step by step as I have explained in this brief explanation.

Screw back cover cases were less expensive to manufacture. That is why hunting cases usually cost double the open face cases.

"Markings and Test Procedures"

There are many books written on watch case markings. Most of them list names and trade mark pictures. But, to understand their meaning is a jungle all of its own. The British trade marks of a particular metal content are more readily available. American trade marks seem to be more confusing. I will only touch on a few marks. The following are gold filled marks: "Monarch 14K"; "Excelsior"; "Olympia"; "The Yacht"; "Chamtion"; "Criterion"; "Banner'; "Manerva"; "Peerless"; "Sport"; "Timekeeper"; "Star"; "Diplomat"; "Mercury"; "Pilgrim"; "Tempus"; "Argyle"; "Solar"; "Lenox"; and "Imperial".

These are among a few of the thousands of names of watch cases manufacturers today. They range from 5 to 15 years. Very seldom marked, with less than a 20 year guarantee. Once in a while I have come across gold-filled cases marked 5,10 and 15 years-but, very, very seldom. Only the 20 year and 25 year cases were marked because of their high quality.

To my surprise most collectors will call nice gold filled cases 20 years, when they are not. Some day this will make a big difference in the pricing of a watch. Some cheaper quality gold filled cases are not gold on the inside covers.

The best way to tell the number of years that a case has had is when the brass shows through the edge of the rim or case cover. If it shows brass, there has been 10 years wore off the case on a 20 year case.

Engraving is another way to tell, but not always true, as in some cases the engraving was made very light and some very heavy.

Many sterling and coin silver cases were made, but they were not as popular as gold filled. Basic cost of silver at the time prohibited silver cases in favor of gold filled cases. Gold filled cases were more beautiful. In order to make strength in silver they had to use as much as 8 ounces in hunting cases. So, the basic intrinsic value was high to start with. This was why we became the greatest gold filled case manufacturers in the world.

If a person wanted to protect his watch movement and use his watch daily, he would more than likely buy a nickel, silveroid, silverine or Alaska silver case. They were similar in color to silver. Although they contain 54½ copper, 45½ nickel and 1½ manganese. From my experiences I have found more 21J and 23J railroad watches in these cases in Canada. Canadians seemed to use these cases a lot more because of the life style of Canada at the time.

Now, concerning the testing of solid gold cases — I am going to explain this in three basic steps.

Step 1 — Always scratch, with a knife, on the inside cover near the cover hinges. Step 2-Use a drop, of nitric acid on the scratch. If it bubbles green from out of the scratch it is the action on the brass between the layers of gold. Sometimes the plate will be very heavy and you can be fooled. So, give it a further test by scratching harder being careful not to mar or damage the case. Step 3 — This is the secret to it; one which of gold itself. Gold is one of the most malleable, colorful and heat conductive metals known to man. Gold is also a very heavy metal. These are some of the reasons why man has used gold as money and ornamentation since the beginning of civilization. Now, if you don't have acid at the time you buy a watch, give it the heat and cold test. Take a known gold filled case (either gold filled or hunting) and hold it to your cheek, and time how long it takes it to warm to the body temperature of your face. Then do the same with the unknown watch, if it's gold there should be some difference. A gold filled case never feels to be completely warm on the cheek. Up to maybe one hour solid gold will always warm up to body temperature. This is why some "old timers" say they can tell the gold by the feel. Some test for softness by biting into it with their teeth. Some claim they can even smell and taste real gold, but, I could never pass this test.

Testing For Carat Content After You Have Established That It Is Gold:

Watch cases were made in the following karats: 7K, 9K, 12K, 14K, and 18K. I have never seen higher than 18K gold cases, but, there may be some British ones around.

Without taking a course in chemistry, I think this would be the best novice procedure:

9K Drop of Nitric Acid-turns brown quickly.
14K Turns brown within one minute.
18K will repel Nitric Acid like water from a rain coat. It will take up to 12 hours to turn brown.

I hope that you have enjoyed this article and happy hunting.

A Horological Note:

The city of Waltham, Massachusetts is famous for its watch companies.

There seems to have been some difficulty between the Waltham Watch Company and the U.S. Watch Company of Waltham.

Either through a lawsuit or a threat of a suit, there is an inscription on the plates of some U.S. Watch Company watches stating ''A New Watch Company in Waltham''.

This seems to have made everyone reasonably happy. If not happy, at least peaceful!

ON THE BALL: A Short History Of The Ball Watch Company; And Webb C. Ball's Involvement In Railroad Timekeeping.

On April 19, 1891 there was a tremendous head-on collision of two trains in the Lake Shore and Michigan Southern Railroad near Kipton, Ohio. This railroad mishap had far reaching effects on both watch production and railroad timekeeping in the U.S.

Other railroads were becoming involved in improvements in railroad timekeeping, but Webb C. Ball's services to the Vanderbilt Railroads were to lead the way in the establishment of standardized railroad timekeeping.

There was indeed a definite need for more accurate timekeeping on American railroads. This need was not only well demonstrated by a series of railroad accidents, but by the appearance of fast passenger trains in the last decade of the nineteenth century. By 1893 the New York Central and Hudson River Railroad had passenger trains that could travel better than 100 miles an hour.

It is not surprising that there were difficulties on the railroads when you consider the fact that time was told on such varied timepieces as the dollar watch and alarm clocks. Such unstandardized use resulted in several trains being in the wrong place at the wrong time, resulting in much property damage and some loss of life. Now, with the arrival of the fast passenger train, something had to be done and quickly.

The before mentioned crash on the Lake Shore and Michigan Southern Railroad is generally conceded to be the beginning of Webb C. Ball's involvement in railroad timekeeping.

Before 1902 the Lake Shore and Michigan Southern Railroad had its headquarters in Cleveland, Ohio. Conveniently the headquarters of the Ball Watch Company was also in Cleveland. It is not clear whether the railroad company went to Mr. Ball, or Mr. Ball went to the railroad with his ideas. And it matters little, when you consider the results of the union.

Ball's first project was to inspect the available watches being used on the LS & M.S. Railroad. Better than 2300 watches were inspected with more than 450 rejections.

These 450 plus rejections meant 450 plus possibilities for railroad accidents based on bad watches alone. Obviously, this was not good!

The only solution was the use of higher quality watches. As railroad watch collectors know, some of the requirements for railroad watches were eventually to be: Open face; 19 jewels, (or more); adjusted to 5 or more positions; and lever set. These requirements came about gradually. In fact in the very beginning Hunting cased watches were acceptable. Position requirements came late in the railroad watch development period.

The following watch companies made railroad quality watches for the Ball Watch Company; Howard; Elgin; Hampden; Hamilton; Waltham, and Illinois.

After his first, and very revealing, inspection Ball established agents to inspect and sell watches in most railroad towns. The Ball Watches were marked Ball Watch Co. on the dial and back plate.

The Hamilton Watch Company made a watch with the grade #999, this was made for Ball. The #999 was not only likely not a Hamilton number, but a Ball number, but it apparently had an association with engine #999 of the NYC&HR Railroad that set the speed record of more than 110 miles an hour in 1893.

The collector will find that some Hamilton Balls were signed with the name of local watchmakers who were likely authorized agents and inspectors of the Ball Watch Company.

By 1902 Webb C. Ball was in charge of railroad time inspection on all Vanderbilt railroads east of Chicago. By this date Ball's timekeeping standards and inspection service had arrived at maturity. Fast trains now ran with safety and precision that were a direct result of Webb C. Ball's dedication to standardization and inspection. It is safe to say that the fast passenger trains of the day could not have existed without standard timekeeping. It is also difficult to imagine today's dependable railroad freight service without precise timekeeping standards. Mr. Ball's contribution to railroad development and U.S. watch production was by no means a small one! His railroads were really "ON THE BALL"!

A SHORT HISTORY OF DIETRICK GRUEN
AND THE GRUEN WATCH.

1924 was a big year at the Gruen Watch Factory in Cincinnati, Ohio. It was the 50th anniversary of the Gruen's involvement in watchmaking and they were making a special presentation model to celebrate the event.

Back in 1867 Dietrick Gruen was visiting his brothers, who had migrated from Germany and had settled in Ohio. He had spent some time with his two brothers and was now ready to return to Germany. Dietrick Gruen was not to return home.

What happened? A pretty face, what else! He met and married in 1869 Pauline Wittlinger. His brothers talked him into staying in this country and he got a job as a watchmaker.

After several years experience he came to believe that there was an excellent opportunity for the development of the watch industry in this country. So, in 1874, he started his own watchmaking factory in Columbus, Ohio.

Mr. Gruen was completely sold on the idea of the production of a quality timepiece. His first watches appeared in 1875, they were 18s, stem wind, lever set, 3/4 plate and fully jeweled. In 1875 he was producing 10 watches a day, but his production was to increase greatly due to the great demand.

Dietrick Gruen's watches were made up of parts made in Switzerland and assembled in his Columbus, Ohio plant at Broad and High Streets. Due to frequent trips to Switzerland and the manufacturing as well as selling aspects of the business, Gruen was forced to take on a partner in 1879. The partner was William J. Savage, and the firm became known as Gruen and Savage.

In 1880, they began the manufacture of quality 16s and 8s movements. These were added to the 18s line of watches. Demand still increased, so they expanded to a new factory at New and Thurman Streets in Columbus.

On November 18, 1882 the Columbus Watch Company was established with capital of $150,000 with Dietrick Gruen as President and W.J. Savage as Secretary and Treasurer. The first movements were turned out in 1883. The 18s, 16s, and 8s watches were continued, but new grades were added.

By 1885 the company had expanded to employ 125 people. By 1891 there were 300 people employed and the daily production of watches had increased to 150 per day.

Young Fred Gruen was to enter the business about this time. Unfortunately the panic of 1893 also hit the watch company very hard at this time. Watches were items that people could do without in extremely hard times.

The big watch companies like Waltham and Elgin began to cut prices. This was more than the smaller companies like the Columbus Watch Co. could stand. It effected the Columbus Watch Company so badly that they were forced into receivership in 1894. This was not only a complete reverse in the fortunes of the company, but also in the fortunes of the Gruens. But, the old adage "that you cannot keep a good man down" now becomes evident.

Gruen and son Fred got together and organized a partnership known as "D. Gruen & Son". In 1895, the first movements were assembled in Cincinnati from parts made in Dresden, Germany.

In 1895, another son, George, entered the company. George was to take care of the financial end of the business, Fred the sales and father the technical end of the enterprise. By 1900, the organization was running smoothly and showing a very good profit, so the Gruens were able to pay off their debts.

Between 1902 and 1904 the Gruens phased out their Dresden connection and began getting all their parts from Switzerland.

The Gruens developed direct contact with the retail jeweler trade. In fact, Fred Gruen traveled all over the U.S., Canada and Mexico selling the watches.

In 1904, the Gruen "Verithin" model was introduced, but was not very popular at first. There were some mechanical problems. By 1908 however, the problems had been solved and the model began to show a profit.

The Gruens were excellent salesmen. They issued their watches in attractive boxes with nice warranty certificates. Their advertising methods were also excellent. This coupled with the fact that they insisted that they produce only quality watches, made the Gruen Company very, very successful!

Generally, it was the know-how, the willingness to make their ideas work, and the determination of the Gruens that made their watch production enterprise a success.

A HISTORY OF THE ILLINOIS WATCH COMPANY

The Illinois Watch Company was organized in January of 1869. They made watches from 1872 to 1927 and were big American watch companies from 1890 to 1910. They specialized in the high quality seven to 24 jeweled, three to six adjusted position movements. They manufactured movements in Springfield, Illinois, and carried on business from offices in Chicago and New York. The company went through two transitional stages before becoming the Illinois Watch Company. They were the Illinois Springfield Watch Company and the Springfield Illinois Watch Company.

Illinois Springfield Watch Company was organized in January of 1869 by J. C. Adams. They opened up their factory in Springfield, Illinois. They manufactured their first keywind watch in 1872 and their first stemwind in 1875. The company reorganized in 1875 with B. M. Bates replacing T. J. Stuart as president of the firm. It reorganized in 1879 as the Illinois Springfield Watch Company.

The original Board of Directors were officers: T. J. Stuart - president, W. B. Miller - secretary. Other members of the board were: J. W. Bunn, G. Passfield, J. Williams, and G. Black. Superintendents were: J. K. Bigelow from 1870 to 1873; D. G. Currier from 1873 to 1875; Otis Hoyt from 1875 to 1878; C. B. Mason from 1878 onward. In 1878 or 1879, due to internal dissention, both Currier and Hoyt left the Illinois company and joined the staff at Waltham Watch Company.

Springfield Illinois Watch Company manufactured watches from 1879 to 1885. Officers were: Jacob Bunn - president, J. W. Bunn - vice president. There were twelve other members of the Board of Directors.

They opened an office in New York and F. Cory was the first agent. L. Arnold replaced J. M. Morrow as the agent in Chicago. They reorganized in 1885 as the Illinois Watch Company.

The Illinois Watch Company manufactured watches from 1885 to 1927. They bought out Aurora Watch Company in 1892 and supplied parts to the W. C. Ball Watch Company in 1900. They also made watches for the Burlington Watch Company, the Washington Watch Company, and the Sears and Roebuck Watch Company.

Eighteen men were employed in thirteen positions. The

positions were mechanics, balance adjustments, plates, gilding, screws, pinions, pinion cutting, accuracy timing, jewels, assembly of the stemwinding mechanism, escapements, dials, and finish.

The Illinois Watch Company was sold to the Hamilton Watch Company in 1927, but the factory continued until 1933. In 1933 the factory was closed, fifty percent of the equipment was sold in Springfield and the rest of the equipment was taken to Hamilton. Hamilton completed and sold the remaining movements until 1939.

They first manufactured keywind watches, these are the common characteristics. They are size 18 movements, housed in silveroid hunting or open face cases. Open face watches had a hinged bezel so it could be removed to set the hands. All movements were 15 jewels. Model names of these watches were Stuart, Miller, Bunn, Currier, Allis, and Hoyt. One keywind was listed in the movement catalog of the company as the Railroader and is easily identifiable by the locomotive and coal car on the reverse plate.

Illinois made ladies' watches that were keywind also. They were six size, housed in hunting cases, and were 15 jewel movements. Model names of these watches were the Allington and the Mary Stuart.

Illinois made some movements that were known as transitionals. Transitionals were a very rare and unique type of watch, as they could either be wound or set by the stem or by a key. Transitionals were found in all the previously mentioned size 18 movements.

The Illinois Company made three major types of watches. They were Railroad, Men's Dress, and Ladies' Pendant watches.

Qualifications, for a watch to be used in railroad service were: have at least a 19 jewel movement, adjusted in no less than five positions, stem be at the twelve o'clock position, and possess a bold Arabic numeral dial.

Illinois made some of the best railroad watches ever manufactured. I will devote a listing and characteristics of each watch.

The highest quality Illinois watch for railroad use was the Sangamo Special. This watch was 16 size, 23 ruby and sapphire jewels, skeletonized movement, adjusted in six positions. This watch had the distinct characteristic of being the only watch to be sold as a complete watch. A sister movement, named the Sangamo, was also a railroad watch and it had a 21 jewel movement.

The Bunn family was composed of five types of watches. All were 18 or 16 size and ranged from 17 to 24 jewel movements. The highest quality Bunn contained a six adjusted position balance and 24 jewels and this was a full plate movement. There were three varieties of the Bunn Special, these watches were either ¾ or full plate movements. The varieties were a 23 jewel with a 60 hour mainspring, a 23 jewel with a 30 hour mainspring, and a 21 jewel model. The Bunn was a 19 jewel model, although railroad approved it, it was frowned on by some railroad watch inspectors.

The last two types are classified as railroad watches because of the 21 jewel movements. These are the Illinois Special and the Santa Fe Special.

Illinois specialized in mostly men's dress watches. They made some of the best quality movements comparable to no other watch.

The A. Lincoln was a popular watch of the early 1900's. There were three varieties of the watch. They were the Barrister, Pioneer, and Acorn. These were distinguishable by the face and case difference. These are 12 size, 19 jewel, adjusted in five position movements.

Illini was the best quality men's watch that Illinois made. They were 21 jewel movements and were adjusted in three positions. There are four varieties of faces and cases.

The Autocrat was another popular watch and was extremely common. It was a 12 size, 17 jewel movement. There are three varieties of faces and cases.

The Marquis Autocrat was another one of the better quality watches. It was a 17 jewel, adjusted in three positions movement. There are two varieties of faces and cases.

The next type of watches were more work watches than dress watches. They are usually found in heavy 20 year gold plated cases, in both hunting and open face varieties.

The Special was one of the higher quality work watches. It was a 12 size, adjusted in three positions, 19 jewel movement.

The Bunn is from the same family as the railroad watches of the same name. Being only a 17 jewel watch it was ineligible for railroad service. It was adjusted in five positions and had a ¾ plate movement.

The Sangamo was another watch with a railroad family history, but for some unknown reason it was not approved for railroad service. It was a 19 jewel movement and was adjusted in six positions. Among collectors it is occasionally grouped with railroad watches.

Illinois made a series of watches that were given numerical identification. The only movements that had the numbers stamped on them were the 555 and 706. The rest are identifiable only by movement characteristics.

The 555 and 706 are the only movements that have the numerical identification. The characteristics of both are the same which leads me to believe that the 555 is a fore runner of the 706. They are 16 size movements, 17 jewel and adjusted in four positions.

The 305 and 405 are the same type movements, except the 305 is 16 size and the 405 is a 12 size. Otherwise they are 17 jewel, skeletonized movements.

The 410 was the highest grade of these watches and could be classified as a railroad watch. This watch could be bought as a 23 or 21 jewel watch and was adjusted in six positions with a skeletonized movement.

Illinois manufactured watches for two other companies. They were the Burlington Watch Company and the Washington Watch Company.

For Burlington there were two models. The Burlington Special, which was 16 size, 21 jewels and the Burlington, which was 12 size and 19 jewels.

There were four varieties made for the Washington Watch Company. They were all 18 size. They were: Lafayette - 24 jewels, Army - Navy - 19 jewels, and the Liberty Bell and Senate - both 17 jewels.

Illinois made Ladies' Pendant watches in 6, 3, 0, 3/0 size. They all carry Illinois Watch Company, Springfield, Illinois. They are seven to 21 jewel and are extremely scarce.

The Illinois Watch Company would probably be in business today if a change in dress style had not taken place. After World War I the wrist watch had gained popularity and by 1930 forced pocket watches into oblivion. Illinois made quality pocket watches only equal to those made by the Hamilton Watch Company, the company that bought them out.

THE PHILADELPHIA WATCH COMPANY (1868-1886)

Eugene Paulus died in Geneva, Switzerland on May 29, 1892. He was a native of Paris and had served in the French Army. In 1852 he came to America and practiced his trade of watchmaking in New York and other cities. In 1868 he settled in Philadelphia and organized the Philadelphia Watch Company and became it s president. He was a master watchmaker adding several improvements to his watches and registering several patents on his improvements.

The first manufacturing took place at 714 Chestnut Street in Philadelphia. Between 1874 and 1880 the company address was 618 Chestnut Street and finally in 1880 it was again changed. From 1880 to 1886 the address was 806 Chestnut Street. 1886 was the last year of production.

The first and last years were not too productive, but, there were 10,000 to 12,000 movements made in 16 years of manufacturing. This was a good record considering the company was never really a large manufacturer and their movements were handmade.

Hand manufacture is evident by the presence of scribe marks and file marks on the movements. Of course, some of these marks were subsequently removed during the manufacturing process. There were also up to 5 punch marks on the movement which indicated the daily production of up to 5 pieces. The serial numbers were listed consecutively.

The Philadelphia Watch Co. made movements only. Cases for the movements were made by G. Gigon Company located nearby in Philadelphia. The cases were of high quality.

Philadelphia Watch Co. made movements in the following sizes: 6, 8, 10, 15, 16, 19, and 20 size. The movements were either gilt or nickel.

The watches were sold by the J. E. Caldwell Company of Philadelphia and by Tiffany and Company of New York. These firms had a reputation for quality merchandise and most certainly would not have handled Philadelphia Watch Company watches if they had not been of the highest quality.

There has been considerable discussion concerning whether or not the Philadelphia Watch Co. made their own movements or had the parts made in Europe and assembled them in the Philadelphia plant. The fact that J. E. Caldwell Co. purchased only from the manufacturer would lead one to believe that the watch was made entirely in Philadelphia. It is difficult to believe that they would have handled "Swiss Fakes". On the other hand, there has been discovered a set of invoices from Europe to the Philadelphia Watch Co. for a shipment of watch parts.

The reader will, of course, have to decide for himself where the truth lies in this matter. It is possible that some of the parts were made in Europe and it is equally possible that all of the parts were made in Europe. Of course, it is possible that all of the parts were made in the U.S. It is hoped that some reader will be interested enough to research this matter fully and make a final conclusion.

The uncertainty of the origin of the watch movement parts does not detract from the fact that the Philadelphia Watch Company made quality handmade watches. The workmanship of these watches showed a pride of workmanship not always evident today with our mass production methods. It is another example of being able to look to our past with a great deal of pride in our American manufacturing methods. I for one, still believe that the pride of workmanship and the free enterprise system are still very much alive in this country.

SIZES OF WATCHES

In American the system of sizing comes from the Lancashire gauge. This is the standard used by watch Mfgrs. in the U.S., starting from 1 inch for the 0-0. The smallest to adding 1/30 of an inch for the next higher size. The following will give you an idea of the size of your watch, by measuring the dial as follows:

0 size	1-5/30 inches	14 size	1-19/30 inches
6 size	1-11/30 inches	16 size	1-21/30 inches
8 size	1-13/30 inches	17 size	1-22/30 inches
10 size	1-15/30 inches	18 size	1-23/30 inches
12 size	1-17/30 inches	20 size	1-25/30 inches

WATCH BOOK TERMS

Pos. see page 10	Positions
O.F.	Open face case
H.	Hunting case
J.	Number of jewels
s. Like in 6s, 12s etc...	Size of watch
G.F.	Gold Filled
6/12s, 0/16s or 12/14s	Size of movement cased into a larger size case.
	Example: 6 size movement in a 12 size case.
K.W.	Keywind watch
N	Nickel case, Silverine, or Silveroid
S	Sterling silver case or coin case
K.S.	Key set

Adams & Perry Watch Mfg. Co., Lancaster, Pa., 1874-1875
Financial crisis caused the company to fail. It was reorganized
as the Lancaster Watch Company in 1877.

				Buy	Sell
Rare	15J	18s	O.F.	$4400	$4600

American Horology Co., 1850
  (See Howard, Davis & Dennison)

Ansonia Watch Co., Brooklyn, N.Y., 1850
The company started manufacturing clocks in 1850. Made
dollar watches inscribed on back plates, patented April 17,
1888.

Appleton Watch Co., Appleton, Wis., 1887

Semi-scarce	18s	G.F., O.F.	$ 350	$ 375

Used parts from the Cheshire Watch Company. The cases were
made special by the company for these movements. This
watch case is a collector's item itself. The stem is connected
to the movement and lifts out from the front.

Auburndale Watch Co., Auburndale, Mass., 1879-1883
This was the first attempt to produce a dollar watch. Inventor
of this revolving watch was J. R. Hopkins. Watches were
known as "Auburndale Rotary" and the later chronograph
model was known as the "Auburndale Timer".

Rare	18s	S.H.	$1450	$1550

Atlas Watch Co., Chicago, Ill.

Semi-common	18s	O.F.N.	$ 75	$ 85

Aurora Watch Co., Aurora, Ill., 1883-1892
Output of this company was sold to retailers the first two years
and then after this period was sold on the open market. The
machinery was sold to the Hamilton Watch Company when
Aurora failed.

Semi-scarce	18s	G.F., O.F.	$ 145	$ 170
	6s	G.F.H.	255	285
Keywinds	18s	S.H.	275	310
		14K Box Case	1000	1100
	18s	G.F.H.	300	330

Boston Watch Co., Roxbury, Mass., 1853-1857
Made approximately 750 watches, the name of Samuel Curtis
appears on the plates.
Very Rare

Ball Watch Co., (See page 72)

Bannatyne Watch Co., Waterbury, Conn., 1905-1911
Made dollar watches that sold for $1.50.

Benedict & Burnham Co., Waterbury, Conn., 1855
The parent company of Waterbury Watch Company. In 1870 the name was Benedict & Burnham Manufacturing. Now it is the American Brass Company. The first 1,000 watches had this name on the dial.

			Buy	Sell
Rare	18s	O.F.	$4500	$5000

Boston Watch Co., Roxbury, Mass., 1852-1857
Made about 700 watches bearing the name Samuel Curtis.

Bristol Watch Co., Bristol, Conn., 1900
Not much is known about this company but the firm did make some watches. I have seen a few Swiss imitations. I have seen only the old catalog pictures of this watch. So beware of the cheap Swiss imitations.

Very scarce	18s	O.F.S.	$ 225	$275
Keywinds	18s	O.F.S.	275	300

Bowman Watch Co., Lancaster, Pa., 1877-1882
A retail jeweler, Ezra Bowman, formed this company with the factory above his retail store. He produced and marketed an excellent watch, employing only five persons. Unfortunately the watch proved to be very expensive to produce, leaving a small margin of profit. Subsequently, he quit the watch business and went back to retail. The plant was sold to the J. P. Stevens Company of Atlanta, Ga.

Rare			$2800	$3400

Burlington Watch Co., (See III.)

California Watch Co., Berkeley, Calif., 1876-1878
Formerly Cornell Watch Company of San Francisco. Closed because of lack of capital. The plates of the movements are the same as the Cornell companies. The machinery was sold to the Fredonia Watch Company.

Rare			$1750	$1950

1. Appleton Watch Co., Appleton, Wisc.

2. Bristol W. Co., Keywind, from the Ronald Bristol Collection

3. Ill. Hoyte, Keywind

4. Rockford, Keywind, #15,526

5. Home W. Co. K.W.

6. Queen City W. Co., K.W.

7. E.A. Read, Marion, N.J.

8. Wm. Ellery, Boston, K.W.

9. Columbus Watch Co.

10. Columbus Railway King, H.

11. California Watch Co., 18s, K.W.

12. Ball Watch Co. W. 19J 16 size

13. Cornell Watch Co., George Root model

14. Cornell, O.F. Bowen model

15. Cheshire Watch Co.,
Cheshire, Conn.

16. Elgin Watch Co.,

B. W. Raymond

21J late model

17. Elgin 6s, Dutchess model

18. Elgin varitas style plates 12s

19. 14K, 12s, made for Rice University

20. Elgin 16s, convertible

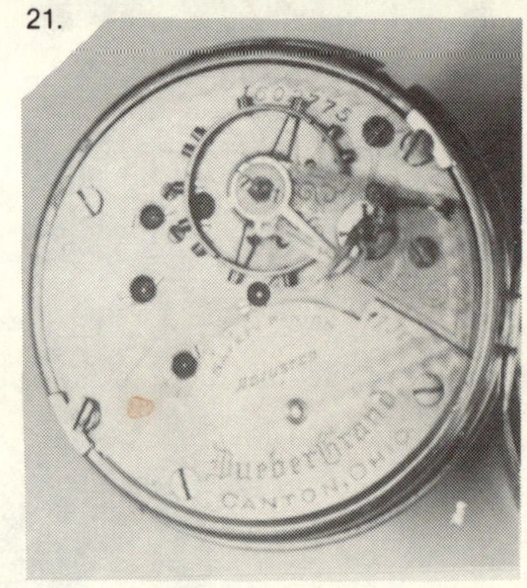

21. Dueber Grand, Hampden

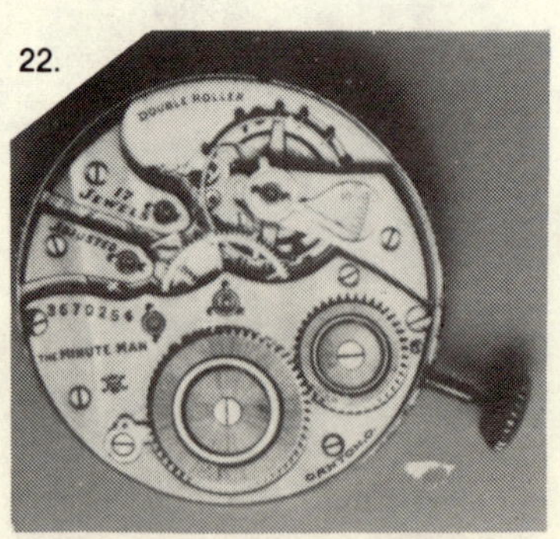

22. The Minute Man

23. Railway 23J, 18s

24. Dueber 16J scarce,
from the Howard Brumley Collection

25. Hamilton Railway Special

26. Rare Hamilton 7J, 18s

27. 993, H., 16s

28. 961, 21J, 16s, H.

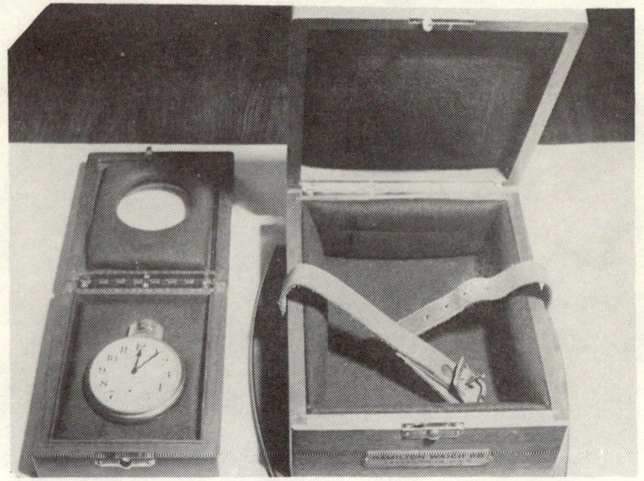

29. Hamilton ship chronometer with up and down indicator.

30. 12 size, 19J model 900 in 14K gold

31. Howard series 3, K.W.

32. 18s Howard N series

33. Howard 6s, G series

34. Howard series 11, chronometer, 21J

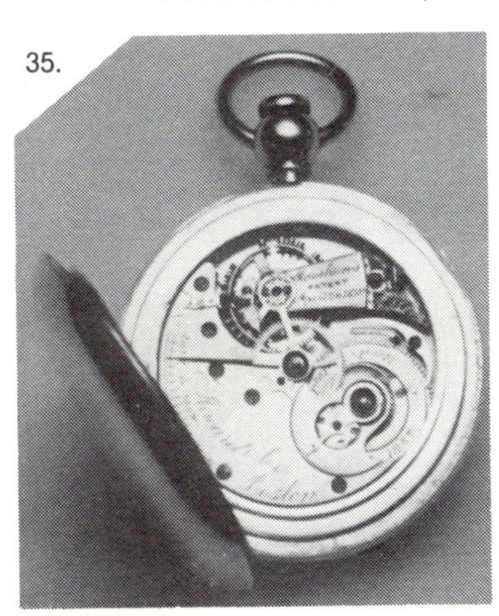

35. Howard series 1,

1859-Mershons pat.

rack lever regulator,

from the

Howard Brumley Collection

36. Howard 16s, 19J, series 5

37. Dennison, Howard and Davis,
18 size, K.W.

38. A. Lincoln, 21J, 16s

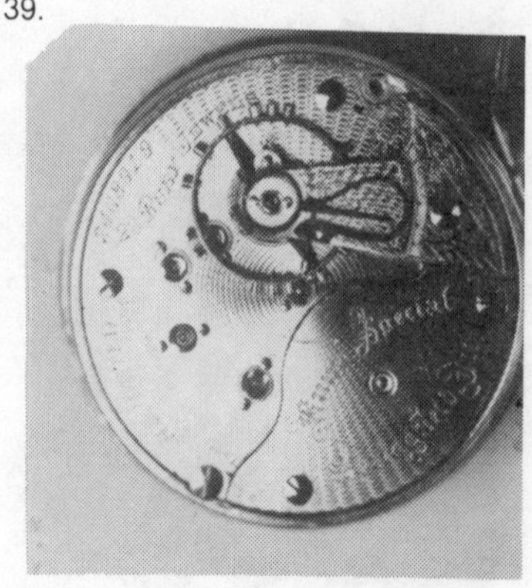

39. Bunn Special 18s, 23J

40. A. Lincoln 21J, 18s

41. Bunn Special 21J, 16s

42. Illini 21J, 5P, 12s

43. Santa Fe Special 21J with original case

44. Sangamo 21J, 16s

47. Illinois with Ferguson dial

45. The Washington Watch Co.,

24 Ruby jewels, missing

in many watch collections,

Lafayette model

46. Senate model, 17J

48. George Washington, K.W. model

49. Time King 17J, 16s

50. Melrose Watch Co., Boston K.W.

51. U.S. Watch Co., G.A. Read model

52. U.S. Watch Co., George Channing
model, 18s, with butterfly movement
19J, rare

53. Manistee W. Co., Manistee, Mich.,
16s, H.

54. Non-magnetic W. Co., 16s, 15J

55. Keystone W. Co., 18s with dust
cover over the balance

56. Otay, 18s, F.A. Kimball model,
from the Adrian Blades Collection

57. Box case Otay, Kimball model,

this is only the fifth one I have

ever seen. The picture I took

of this watch was in a dimly

lighted place.

58. New York Watch Co., Springfield,
Mass., John Hancock model

59. New England Watch Co.,
duplex escapement

60. The American General,
New England Watch Co.

61. Peoria Watch Co.,
anti-magnetic model 15J, 18s

62. Philadelphia Watch Co.,
very scarce, looks
like an early Howard

63. J. P. Stevens, Atlanta, Ga.

64. Rockford Winnebago
model 17J, 16s

65. 8s Ladies' Rockford

66. Beautiful Damaskeening
on Rockford 18s plates

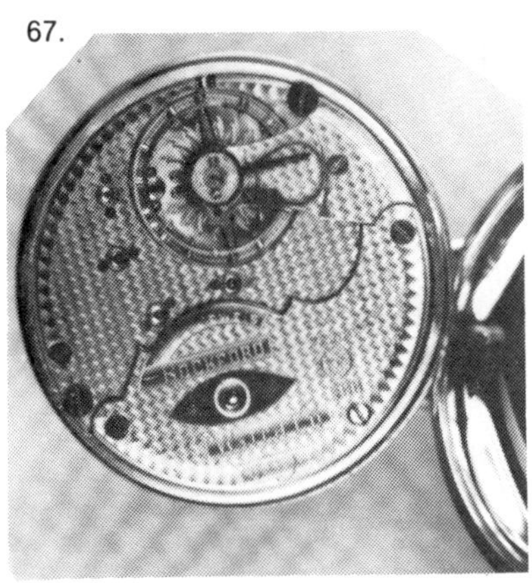

67. Rockford, RG grade, 24J, 18s

68. Rockford, 21J, 18s, RG grade

69. Seth Thomas 18s, 15J, personalized
name of G.W. Bishop.
Compare plates with #69a.

69a. Seth Thomas low serial number,
from the Al Asher collection.

70. Seth Thomas, Maiden Lane, 25J, 18s. The most scarce and sought after of railroad watches.

71. Seth Thomas, 18s with skeletonized movement

72. South Bend Watch Co., Studebaker 16s, 21J

73. #203 7J, 16s

74. The Studebaker, 21J, 18s

75. 12s, 19J, #429

76. 6s, H., 15J, South Bend

77. 9J, 16s, #209 South Bend

78. U.S. Watch Co., Waltham, 18s,
15J, O.F. common

79. U.S. Watch Co., N.Y.,

but same as Waltham, H.,

16s, 15J

80. U.S. Watch Co., but a rare model. Notice the screw at the balance regulator, in order to get the stem out, this screw had to be turned 180 degrees, this would disengage the stem and it could be removed. Many jewelers in the last 25 years have torn up the stems. This has made the model more scarce.

81. Black dial model of U.S. Watch Co., 18s, Hunting

82. Very rare, Waltham's first attempt at engineering a new railroad watch. This is the forerunner of the Vanguard series. Called Waltham's railway timekeeper, 15J, 18s, brass plates. Most sought after by railroad collectors, from the collection of Dave Burdock.

83. Waltham, Adams St., gold keywind,
8s, from Howard Brumley Collection

84. Colonial Maximus, 23J, 14K, O.F.,
12s, Ron Bristol Collection

85. 16A Waltham 16s, made about
1940, belonged to my uncle
Cam Shaw, from Glenn Wells Collection

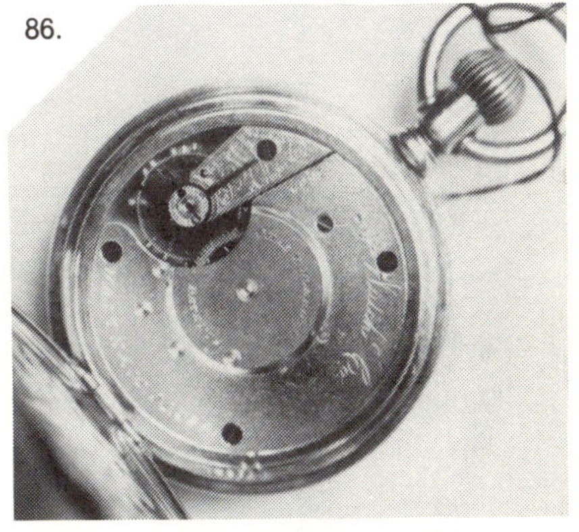

86. U.S. Watch Co., dome model, note
the same kind of stem as #101

87. Waltham Watch Co.,

P.S. Bartlett, 18s, 17J

88. W. W. Co., Royal, 6s, 17J

89. W. W. Co., 16s, Royal, 17J

90. W. W. Co., 16s,

Riverside Maximus,

21J, model 72

91. W. W. Co., 18s, Canadian Pacific, 17J,

made special for Canadian Pacific Railroad

92. 8s, model 73, made for

M.S. Smith & Co., Detroit

93. William Ellery, 8s, Keywind

94. Waltham, 18s, box case with fancy dial

95. 18s, 21J, Vanguard

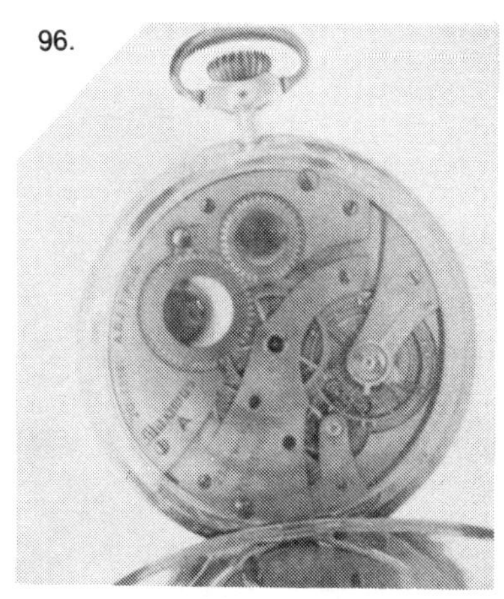

96. Maximus A, 12s, 14K, O.F., 21J

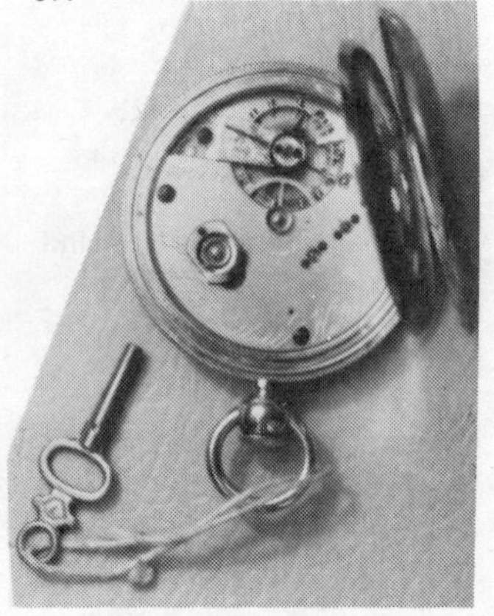

97.

98.

98. Crescent St., 15J, 18s

97. P. S. Bartlett

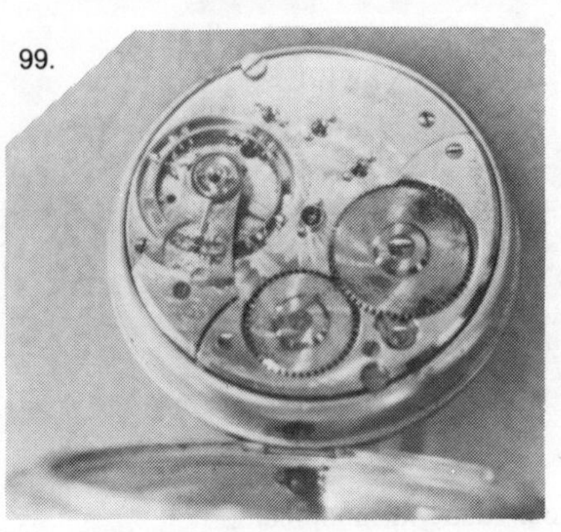

99.

100.

99. Crescent St., 21J

100. Up and down indicator, Waltham

101.

101. 645, 21J, Waltham

102.   102 a

102. Swiss silver dollar watch

103.   103a

103. Swiss imitation of Illinois, Lake Shore, nice Montgomery dial, cheap **works**

104.   105.

104. 16s multi-color   105. 0s Elgin multi-color

106. 16s box case multi-color

107. Burlington Watch,

with 3 engraved horse heads

108. 3 multi-color gold watches

109. Multi-color gold watch
FOB given as a music
award

110. Nielo watch FOB
with compass

111. Vienna Souvenir
Watch FOB, turn
wheel on bottom
and 4 different
scenes appear
in the window
to left.

112. The author and his family in front of the Capitol of the U.S.A.

113. Gold dial eagle watch,

in 18K hunting case

114. Nielo Airplane H. Watch

115. A fine hand painted porcelain dial. Note the tiny scene in the middle of the dial.

116.

116. Montandon Freres of Locle, enamel and ivory inlaid in 18K gold box contains extra parts for watch.

117.

117. 18K gold Demi-Hunter, English made

The following four watches,from the Richard Roy collections.

118.

118. Swiss 8 day calendar watch

119.

119. Button hole watch

120.

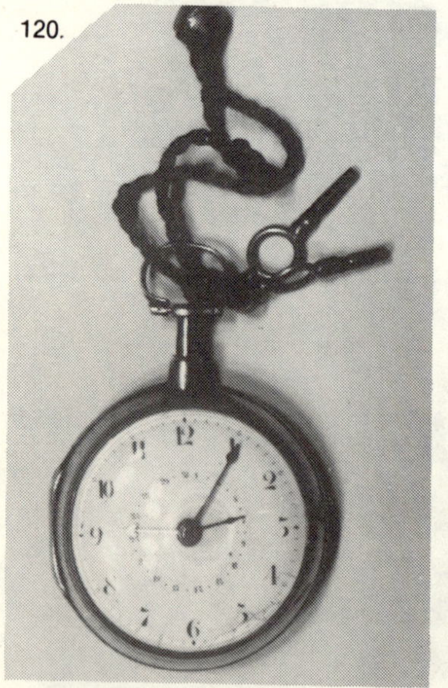

120. Fusee calendar watch,

about 1810

121.

121. Chinese Duplex Watch

123. Longine's gold medal award, Paris 1878

122. Lighter watch, Swiss, 1925

124. Swiss watch made to

commemorate

President Kennedy,

from the

Kay Cook Collection

125. Swiss Keywind with

mother of pearl dial

126. Vacheron-Constantin

silver stop watch, 20J

127. M. J. Tobias, early example

of his fine workmanship.

Notice the large jewels.

128. Example of the finest in

German watchmaking.

M. Grosman.

129. Beautiful scene of a sail boat in Italy.

This type of engraving is called ''Fine Line''

130. More Swiss fine line engraving,

gold dial keywind

131. English silver keywind,

hunting case

132. English silver keywind,

hunting case

133. Tobias, gold dial keywind

134. 18K, gold keywind, Swiss

135. Hampden 21J, H., hand engraved

136. Waltham, 14K, H.

137. South Bend 12s, O.F.

138. Rockford 16s with diamond

139. Waltham 18s, H.

140. Stag on nickel case

141. The famous race horse, Dan Patch

142. Picture of my last edition

Nov., 1977, still available

143. Humming bird in flight,

white 14K Elgin,

from author's collection.

144. Railroad Watch Co., 18s, 17J, made by Webb Ball, Cleveland. Very scarce because Webb Ball changed the name of his company to Ball Watch Co.

145. Hamilton Ball #999, 17J, 18s

The following pictures from the Melvin Dougherty collection.

146. 18s Hamilton Ball

147. Illinois Santa Fe Special, 21J, 16s

148. 18s, "Red Ball Express",

passenger train

149. 12s watch with scene and bird

The following from the Joe Anthony collection.

150. 16s Howard,

21J, Series 11,

chronometer

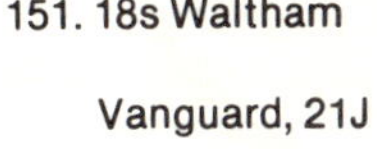

151. 18s Waltham

Vanguard, 21J

152. 18s, Illinois Columbia Keywind, 13J

153. Cornell of Chicago, 18s, George Root model

154. Howard Brumley, "The Ideal Dress"

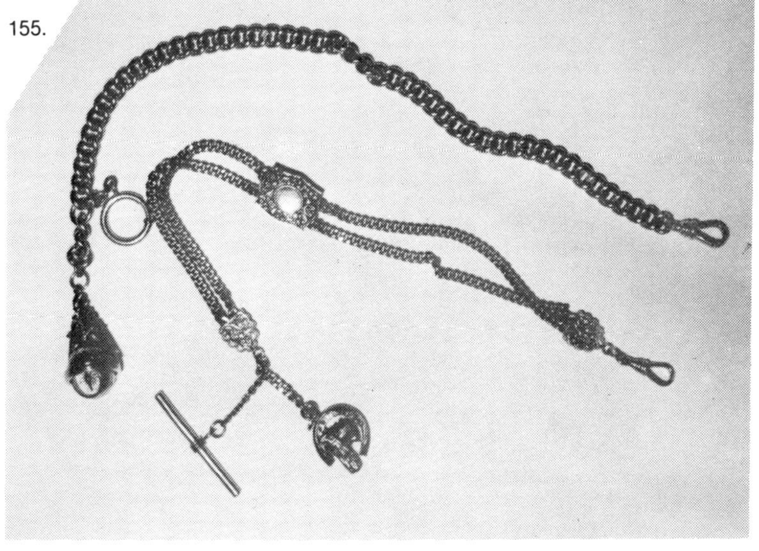

155. Some of H. Brumley's favorite chains

The following watches from the Howard Brumley collection.

156. Non-magnetic Watch Co.

of America, 16s,

14K gold box case

157. 14s Howard,
23J, 14K gold

158. Hamilton Railroad Special,
21J, 992B

159. Howard 18s,

Mersham's patent

April 26, 1859

160. Deluxe 92 hole watch carrying case

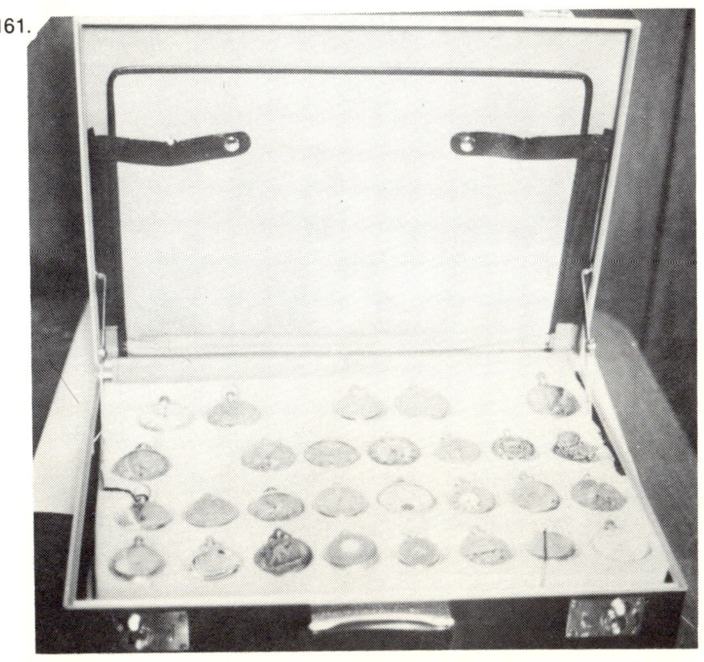

161.   64 hole watch carrying case

162. 31 hole watch carrying case, contact author for details

163. Collection of wrist watches

Cheshire Watch Co., Cheshire, Conn., 1883-1893
D. A. Buck, designer of the "Long Wind" Waterbury watch, was
superintendent of this company for the first three years. Many
models and hundreds of watches, all stem-wind, stem-set,
were made during these ten years. The Cheshire was a well
made watch for only having seven jewels.

				Buy	Sell
Scarce	7J	18s	H.G.F.	$ 300	$345
	7J	18s	O.F., G.F.	210	235
	7J	6s	H.G.F.	255	285

Chicago Watch Co., Chicago, Ill., 1898
Made 7J, open face, silveroid case watches.

			Buy	Sell
7J	18s	O.F.	$ 75	$ 95

Columbia Watch Co., Waltham, Mass., 1896-1901
They made twelve watches and then became Suffolk Watch
Company in 1901. *BEWARE OF SWISS FAKES.*

Columbus Watch Co., Columbus, Ohio, 1882-1903
Business sold to South Bend Watch Company in 1903.

				Buy	Sell
	7J	16s-18s	S.R.,O.F.	$ 60	$ 80
	15J	16s-18s	G.F.,O.F.	95	125

Hunting case 40% more, mint 50% more.

				Buy	Sell
Multi-color gold	14K	16s	H.	1200	1300
Multi-color gold	14K	18s	H.	1800	2100
Box Case	14K	18s	H.	1550	1600

COLUMBUS NAMES

				Buy	Sell
Railway Monarch	17J	18s	G.F.H.	300	350
Time King, rare	14K,25J	18s	O.F.	2000	2100
Time King	21J	18s	O.F.,G.F.	245	275
Time King	23J	18s	O.F.,G.F.	300	345
New Columbus	15J-17J		O.F.,G.F.	85	100
Railroad King	17J	18s	O.F.,G.F.	175	200
Railroad King	21J	18s	O.F.,G.F.	250	275
Keywind		18s	S.H.	400	425
Ladies' type	14K	0s	H.	275	300
Ladies' type		6s	G.F.H.	155	180
North Star		18s	G.F., O.F.	110	130
New Columbus	21J	16s	H.G.F.	295	325
Ruby Model	21J	16s	O.F. or H.	350	450

Fancy Dial Add 50% To Above Prices.

Columbus King, Up and Down

			Buy	Sell
Indicator	18s	O.F.	1800	1900

Cornell Watch Co., Chicago, Ill., 1870-1874

Formerly Newark Watch Company. The following movements were made: Paul Cornell, W. M. Hibbard, C. T. Bowen, C. M. Cody, George F. Root, John Evans, E. S. Williams and George W. Waite Company moved to San Francisco, California, and then became Cornell Watch Company, San Francisco, California.

			Buy	Sell
	18s	N. or S.	$ 850	$900
15J	18s	G.F.,O.F.	850	900
15J	18s	14K H.	1250	1350

Cornell Watch Co., San Francisco, Calif., 1874-1876

After the death of the cashier, who defrauded the company of most of its funds, was organized under the name California Watch Company. The factory moved to Berkeley, California.

Custer, Jacob, Norristown, Pa., 1840-1845

Mr. Custer made 14 size, lever escapements, and clocks. He was the third American watchmaker. I would say this is one of the scarcest watches to find today.

Very, very rare	14K	14s	O.F.	$13,000	$14,000

Dudley Watch Co., Lancaster, Pa., 1893-

Dudley made unusual watches forming the Masonic symbol. All the parts were ordered from the Hamilton Watch Company.

Very scarce	21J	12s	G.F., O.F.	$1200	$1300

Elgin Watch Co., Elgin, Ill., 1864-1951

This was one of the most successful watch companies in the United States for the length of time it was in business. For the first ten years it was known as the National Watch Company. In 1873 the company sold the first stemwind watches. Hundreds of different models were produced.

Comm.-scarce,	17J	18s	O.F.N.	$ 55	$ 65
all sizes	15J	18s	O.F., N.	50	60
	15J-17J	16s	O.F., G.F.	45	55
	7J	18s	O.F., N.	35	45
	21J	16s	O.F., G.F.	95	110
	23J	16s	O.F., G.F.	200	240

Hunting cases 50% more on above watches. Mint, increase 50%.

EARLY KEYWINDS

				Buy	Sell
Serial No. to 5,000			H.	$ 240	$260
5,000 to 10,000			H.	175	200
H.H. Taylor		18s	O.F., N.	105	125
Mat Lafline		18s	O.F., G.F.	125	155
H.L. Culver		18s	O.F., G.F.	105	130
M.D. Ogden		18s	O.F., N.	100	125
J.T. Ryerson		18s	O.F., G.F.	145	165
J.V. Farwell		18s	O.F., G.F.	155	175
Charles Fargo		18s	O.F., G.F.	115	145
T.M. Avery		18s	O.F., G.F.	125	155

Hunting cases 40% increase.

LADIES' KEYWIND DEXTER ST. AND LADY ELGIN MODELS

				Buy	Sell
Scarce,	14K and 10K	8s	H.	$295	$ 350
Strand	17J	12s	4 Pos.	75	95
Railroad Quality Elgins					
162 Bar Movement					
	21J	16s	O.F., G.F.	300	345
Veritas					
	21J	16s	O.F., G.F.	175	210
	23J	16s	O.F., G.F.	295	345
	21J	18s	O.F., G.F.	165	195
	23J	18s	O.F., G.F.	275	310
Father Time					
	21J	16s	O.F., G.F.	155	185
Father Time, full plate					
	21J	18s	G.F.	230	260
Father Time, 3/4 plate					
	21J	18s	G.F.	220	260
Convertible Model					
	15J	16s	O.F., G.F.	125	155
	15J	18s	O.F., G.F.	300	325
	18K, 15J	16s	O.F.	550	600
	14K, 15J	16s	H.	550	600
Up & Down Indicator					
	21J		O.F., G.F.	450	500
	23J		O.F.	550	650
	19J		O.F.	375	425
Multi-color gold					
	14K	18s	H.	1900	2100
	14K	16s	H.	1200	1300
	14K	6s-12s	H.	650	750
Hunting, scarce	16J	6s	H., G.F.	155	175

Multi-color box case

				Buy	Sell
	14K	16s	H.	$ 1550	$ 1650
	14K	18s	H.	2000	2100
	18K	18s	H.	2500	2750
Francis Rubic		10s	O.F., G.F.	135	160
Dexter Street		10s	O.F., G.F.	95	115
Gail Borden		10s	O.F., G.F.	135	155
Dexter Street	14K	10s	H.	375	425
B.W. Raymond, scarce					
	15J	18s	O.F., G.F.	115	145
B.W. Raymond					
	17J	16s	O.F., G.F.	85	95
	21J	16s	O.F., G.F.	120	155
	19J	18s	O.F., G.F.	150	175
	19J	16s	O.F., G.F.	135	165

Hunting cases 40% increase, mint 50% increase.
Lord Elgin, 8 pos.

				Buy	Sell
	14K, 19J	12s	O.F.	165	185
	14K, 21J	12s	O.F.	235	255
	23J	16s	O.F., G.F.	425	465
Ladies' Elgin		0s-6s	G.F., H.	125	145
		0s-6s	O.F., S.	35	45
	14K	0s-6s	H.	275	325
G.M. Wheeler	15J		O.F., G.F.	75	85
	17J		O.F., G.F.	95	110
349	21J	18s	O.F., G.F.	125	145
Qverland	17J	18s	O.F.	125	145
Up and Down Indicator					
		18s	O.F.	650	750
Bar Movement	17J		O.F., G.F.	85	105

Hunting cases 40% increase, mint 40% increase. These prices
are for both 16 and 18 sizes. Fancy Dial add 50% to above
prices.

Equity Watch Co., Boston, Mass.
Made by Waltham Co.

				Buy	Sell
	15J	16s	H.	$ 95	$ 115
	7J	16s	O.F.	60	85

Fasoldt Watch Co., Rome, N.Y., 1849-1861
Made the first fifty watches at Rome and then moved to
Albany, N.Y.

				Buy	Sell
Very rare		18s	O.F., G.F.	$5500	$6000

Fitchburg Watch Co., Fitchburg, Mass., 1875-1878
It is not known if any watches were made. It was closed because of financial failure. Machinery was sold to Cornell Watch Company.

Fredonia Watch Co., Fredonia, N.Y. 1883-1885
Formerly the Independent Watch Company. Sales were very slow and in 1885 the machinery was moved to Peoria, Illinois, and the company formed as the Peoria Watch Company.

				Buy	Sell
Rare	15J	18s	O.F., G.F.	$ 550	$ 650
	17J	18s	G.F., H.	650	700

Freeport Watch Co., Freeport, Ill. 1874-1875
Purchased the machinery from the Rock Island Watch Company. A short time after the machinery was installed in the plant it was destroyed by fire. It is believed that no movements were made before the fire.

Gladiator Watch Company, Springfield, Mass. 1885
This was made by the Hampden Watch Company.

7J	18s	O.F., N.	$ 75	$ 95

Hall, Johas G., Montpelier, Vermont, 1851-1853
Watchmaker that made watches with his name on them. He worked for Howard and Waltham. While at Waltham he designed the first ladies' model watch, 8 size, P.S. Bartlett.

18s	O.F., G.F.	$11,500	$12,500

Hampden Watch Co., Springfield, Mass., and Canton, Ohio, 1876-1930
Formerly the New York Watch Company of Springfield, Mass. It had great measure of success during its ten years of operation. In 1886 it moved to Canton, Ohio. Due to sound management this company sold over 4,000,000 watches. In 1907, Mr. Dueber died and the sales declined. In 1930 the company moved to Russia.

SPRINGFIELD MODELS
With Springfield, Mass., on plates
E. W. Bond, keywind

			Buy	Sell
	18s	O.F., S.	$ 135	$ 155

State Street, keywind

	18s	O.F., S.	110	145

Theo. E. Studley, keywind

	18s	O.F., S.	175	210

J. C. Perry, keywind

	18s	O.F., S.	135	165

Homer Foot, keywind

	18s	O.F., S.	255	290

Gladiator, keywind & stemwind

			75	100

Lafayette, stemwind

	18s	O.F., S.	100	125

John L. King, keywind

	18s	O.F., S.	210	235

Kingman, stemwind

	18s	G.F., H.	125	155
15J	18s	O.F., S.	50	65
15J	16s	O.F., G.F.	45	60
15J	12s	O.F., G.F.	35	45
7J	6s	G.F., H.	125	155
15J	6s	G.F., H.	175	210

HAMPDEN GRADE NAMES
Railway

			Buy	Sell
15J	18s	G.F., H.	225	260
19J	18s	O.F., G.F.	190	225
19J	16s	O.F., G.F.	190	225
21J	18s	O.F., G.F.	175	195
23J	18s	O.F., G.F.	275	295
21J	16s	O.F., G.F.	165	190
23J	16s	O.F., G.F.	295	330

Same price for the Railway Special and new Railway above.
John Hancock

			Buy	Sell
17J	16s-18s	G.F., O.F.	125	155
19J	16s-18s	G.F., O.F.	175	210
21J	16s-18s	O.F., G.F.	175	200
23J	16s-18s	O.F., G.F.	295	330

William McKinley

			Buy	Sell
17J	16s	G.F., O.F.	100	130
19J	16s	G.F.	155	185
21J	16s	G.F., H.	185	210

John C. Dueber

				Buy	Sell
	17J	18s	O.F., G.F.	$ 145	$ 165
	17J	16s	O.F., G.F.	110	135

General C. Stark

	17J	18s	O.F., G.F.	95	120
	21J	16s	O.F., G.F.	145	170
Rare, high jewel	24J ,14K	18s	H., Rare	10,000	11,000

Golden Gate Special

	17J	18s	O.F., G.F.	165	185

Mantilo Park

	17J	18s	O.F.	165	185

Scarce, 16J marked on plates

		18s	O.F., G.F.	225	255

Dueber Grand

	21J	18s	O.F., G.F.	145	175
	21J	16s	O.F., G.F.	135	165
	21J	12s	O.F., G.F.	95	110

Nathan Hale

	21J	12s	O.F., G.F.	95	120

Minute Man

	21J	12s	O.F., G.F.	95	120

Molly Stark

	7J	0s	O.F., G.F.	55	75
	7J	0s	G.F., H.	145	175

Betsy Ross

	7J	0s	O.F., G.F.	65	80
	7J	0s	G.F., H.	145	175

Paul Revere

	15J	12s	O.F., G.F.	95	120

Hampden also made grade numbers.

104	21J	16s	G.F., H.	145	175
104	23J	16s	G.F., H.	225	265
105	21J	16s	G.F., H.	145	165
105	23J	16s	G.F., H.	225	265

Fancy Dial add 75% to above prices.

The above in hunting cases add 50% more. 14K hunting cases, 18s, add 300%. 14K hunting cases, 16s, add 200%. 18K very scarce.

Multi-color gold

	14K	16s	H.	1200	1300
	14K	18s	H.	1800	2100

Multi-color gold, box case

	14K	18s	H.	2000	2100
	18K	18s	H.	2550	2700

Henry and James Watch Co., Pitkin, N.Y.

| | 7J | 16s | KW, KS | | |

Hamilton Watch Co., Lancaster, Pa. 1892-1976

				Buy	Sell
Very rare	7J	18s	O.F.	$ 750	$ 850
	11J	18s	O.F.	750	850
	15J	18s	O.F.	375	400
Common	17J	12s	O.F.	35	45
Hamiltons	17J	16s	O.F.	65	85
No numbers	17J	18s	O.F.	65	85

Hunting cases increase 40%.

Keywind, beware of fakes - rare.

18 Size G.F. Cases

					Buy	Sell
922	15J	O.F.		1,171	550	650
924	17J	O.F.		138,306	55	75
928	15J	O.F.		4,990	375	400
930	16J	O.F.		4,200	350	450
933	16J	HTG.		650	900	1000
936	17J	O.F.		18,336	85	100
939	17J	HTG.		300	1400	1550
940	21J	O.F.		205,815	125	135
941	21J	HTG.		25,411	185	210
942	21J	O.F.		5,418	265	295
943	21J	HTG.		2,399	265	295
944	19J	O.F.		6,600	475	525
946	23J	O.F.		10,682	550	625
947	23J	HTG.		378	4000	4300
948	17J			1,525	195	225
999	19J	O.F.		4,500	300	340
999	21J	O.F.		6,789	290	320
999	23J	O.F.		100		

16 Size

					Buy	Sell
950	23J	O.F.		4,401	375	400
950B	23J	O.F.		4,495	475	525
	23J	O.F. (Elinvar)		7,001	575	625
951	23J	P. or L.				
952	19J	O.F. P. or L.		1,499	475	500
954	17J	P. or L.			155	185
956	17J	P.		51,000	65	85
960	21J	O.F.		3,045	325	360
961	21J	HTG. (Pend. set)		1,152	350	380
961	21J	HTG. (Lever set)		1,100	365	400
963	17J	HTG.		380		
964	17J	P.		325		
966	17J	P.		325		

				Buy	Sell
968	17J	P.	925	$ 250	$ 300
969	17J	HTG.	812	300	350
970	21J	O.F.	2,806	250	275
971	21J	HTG.	2,497	300	350
972	17J	O.F. Railroad Grade	35,652	125	145
973	17J	P.	5,700	85	120
974	17J	L.	218,000	85	100
974B	17J	P. or L.			
975	17J		31,000	75	95
976	16J	O.F.	2,302	295	345
990	21J	O.F.	16,489	145	195
991	21J	HTG.	2,521	200	245
992	21J	O.F. (Pend. set)	3,601	175	200
992	21J	O.F.	104,067	135	150
992B	21J	O.F.	217,876	225	260
992E	21J	O.F.	60,997	165	185
993	21J	HTG.	11,476	225	255
994	21J	O.F.	800	450	500
996	19J	O.F.	23,497	275	300
4992B	22J	O.F. (Gov't. issue)	96,082	125	145
12 Size G.F. Cases					
900	19J	G.F.,O.F.	24,699	45	65
902	14K	O.F.	9,600	150	175
904	21J, 14K	O.F.	4,100	195	220
910	17J	G.F.,O.F.	153,793	45	60
912	17J	G.F.,O.F.	260,900	45	60
914	17J	G.F.,O.F.	43,099	45	60
916	17J	G.F.,O.F.	33,800	45	60
918	19J, 14K	O.F.	17,700	150	175
920	23J, 14K	O.F.	13,598	200	225
922	23J, 14K	O.F.	15,711	200	225
400	21J, 14K	O.F.	2,301	155	175
10 Size G.F. Cases					
917	17J	G.F.,O.F.	152,391	45	65
921	21J	G.F,O.F.	37,749	85	100
923	23J, 14K	G.F.	2,077	175	210
Hamilton Watch Co. 0 Size G.F. Cases					
981	17J	G.F., HTG.	2,200	325	365
983	17J	G.F., HTG.	5,996	325	365
985	19J	G.F., HTG.	1,899	375	410
Hamilton Watch Co. 6/0 Size G.F. Cases					
979	19J	G.F., HTG.	31,800	325	360
986	17J	G.F.,O.F.	55,895	65	85
987	17J	G.F., HTG.	56,895	95	125

Fancy Dial add 100% to above prices on 16s and 18s *ONLY*.

Operas With Diamonds Set In Platinum

				Buy	Sell
12/0		17J	O.F.	$ 1050	$ 1150
14K	16s	17J	H.	495	545
14K	18s	17J	H.	595	650

#22 Deck Watch Chronometer with up & down indicator made for the Navy in the box - 48 hours   450   550

Model 21, Ship's Chronometer Clock   1000   1100

Odds and Ends

				Buy	Sell
Cadillac	16J	16s	O.F., G.F., P.	175	210
Union	17J	18s	O.F., S., L.	125	165
Electric Railway Special					
Pin Set	17J		G.F., O.F.	125	135
Lever Set	17J		G.F., O.F.	125	135

Home Watch Co., Boston, Mass. 1869

Made by the American Watch Co. at Waltham, Mass. When a distributor ordered these watches he could have this name put on the watches. Not too many were made. He could sell them at a lesser price.

				Buy	Sell
Keywind	14K	18s	H.	$ 575	$ 675
Keywind		18s	G.F., H.	225	260
Keywind		18s	S., O.F.	200	235

Howard, Davis & Dennison, Boston, Mass. 1850-1857

This company originated the machine manufacture of watches. Aaron Dennison persuaded Ed Howard to venture into the watch manufacturing business. Operation began at Roxbury, Mass., and later moved to Waltham, Mass. During the following, the life of this company had the following names: 1859 - American Horologe Co., 1853 - Warren Watch Co., Boston Watch Company, Waltham Improvement Co. In 1857 the company failed and was sold to Tracy, Baker and Co.

				Buy	Sell
Keywind models		18s	Silver H.	$ 1450	$ 1550
Keywind models	18K	18s	H.	1750	1850
	14K	18s	Gold H.	1550	1650

Howard, E. & Co., Boston, Mass. 1857-1903

Edward Howard started a new watch company in Roxbury and eventually made the finest watches ever produced in the U.S. In 1903, the rights to the Howard name were sold to the Keystone Watch Case Co. of Philadelphia and they continued under the Howard name until 1930.

1859-1903, Keywind & Stemwind Howards

				Buy	Sell
Series 1	14K	18s	Keywind H	1950	2150
Series 2	14K	18s	Keywind H	1550	1650

				Buy	Sell
Series 3	14K	18s-14s	Keywind H	1550	$ 1650
Series 4	14K	18s	KW/SW	1450	1550
Series 5	14K	16s	KW/SW	1250	1350
Model G.	G.F.	8s	Ladies' H	950	1050
Model G.	14K	8s	Ladies' H	1500	1600
Series 9	G.F.	18s	15J or 17J	375	450
Series 8	G.F.	18s	17J, O.F.	290	330

The following are the most common Howards

				Buy	Sell
	17J	12s	G.F., O.F.	120	145
	17J	16s	G.F., O.F.	175	200
	14K, 17J	12s	O.F.	225	265
	14K, 17J	16s	O.F.	400	450

Keystone Howards, 1903-1930

				Buy	Sell
Series 10	19J	16s	O.F.	275	300
Series 10	21J	16s	O.F.	275	300
Series 10	23J	16s	O.F.	425	460
Series 11	21J	16s	O.F.	225	260
Series 0	23J	16s	O.F.	450	525
Series 0	23J	16s	H.	525	600
Model F., Series 5					
	19J	16s	G.F., O.F.	265	300
Model G., Series 5					
	19J	16s	O.F.	245	275
Model H., Series 5					
	19J	16s	O.F.	225	265
Model K., Series 2					
	17J	16s	O.F.	145	175
Model M., Series 2					
	17J	16s	O.F.	145	175
Model 8A, Z & Y of Series 6					
	19J	12s	O.F.	100	125
Models BB, CC, DD, & EE, Series 7					
	17J	12s	O.F.	100	125
Model R, S, T, & W of Series 8					
	23J	12s	O.F.	175	210
	21J	12s	O.F.	145	175

On some Howard watches you will see a hound, a horse or a deer. This signifies the following:

Hound: Unadjusted

Horse: Adjusted to heat and cold

Deer: Adjusted to temperature and position

The Edward Howard Model

				Sell
Mintage: 275	14K, 23J	16s		$ 9000

Abbott Watch Co., made by Howard Watch Co.
These watches were made so that retail jewelers could sell
them at less than half the Howard price. It was kind of like
being in competition with your own company.

			Buy	Sell
17J	16s	G.F., H.	$ 225	$ 260

Abbott, Sure Time

17J	16s	O.F.,G.F.	175	200
14K, 17J	16s	H.	395	440

Howard Bros. bought parts from several American watch
companies. E. D. and C. M. Howard sold watches for years on
the installment plan. This enterprise failed in 1879.

Howard Bros., Fredonia, N.Y.

Keywind	18s	O.F., N.	$ 650	$ 750

Illinois Springfield Watch Co., Springfield, Ill. 1869-1879
This was the first name of one of the great watch companies in
the U.S. It was commonly known as "The Illinois Watch". The
early watches were all 18 size and named after officials of the
company, such as: Stuart, Bunn, Miller, and Allis. Also, two
ladies' models: Mary Stuart and Arlington. In 1879, the
company was renamed the Springfield Illinois Watch Co.
Keywinds, Semi-scarce

15J	18s	O.F.	$110	$ 145

Transition Models

15J	18s	O.F.	145	175

Common Models

15J	12s	G.F., O.F.	35	45
15J	16s	G.F., O.F.	65	85
17J	18s	G.F., O.F.	75	95
17J	16s	G.F., H.	145	195
17J	18s	G.F., H.	165	200

Beautiful Damaskeen Movements add 25%.

Abe Lincoln	21J	18s	G.F., O.F.	225	250
	21J	16s	G.F., O.F.	175	200
	21J	12s	G.F., O.F.	125	155
	14K, 19J	12s	O.F.	425	465
Sangamo	25J	16s	G.F., O.F.	4000	4500
	23J	16s	G.F., O.F.	325	375
	21J	16s	G.F., O.F.	175	200
	19J	16s	G.F., O.F.	550	600

				Buy	Sell
Sangamo Special	23J	16s	G.F., O.F.	$ 375	$ 425
	21J	16s	G.F., O.F.	210	250
	19J	16s	G.F., O.F.	575	625
Penn. Spec.	24J	18s	G.F., O.F.	950	1050
Diamond, Sapphire or Ruby models					
	23J	16s	G.F., O.F.	550	650
Above add 30% for Hunting Case & Mint 30% more.					
Bunn	15J	16s-18s	G.F., O.F.	225	260
	17J	16s-18s	G.F., O.F.	145	175
	19J	16s-18s	G.F., O.F.	220	225
	21J	16s-18s	G.F., O.F.	175	200
	24J	18s	G.F., O.F.	650	700
	24J	18s	G.F., H.	700	750
Bunn Spec.	21J	16s-18s	G.F., O.F.	145	175
	23J	16s-18s	G.F., O.F.	275	325
	24J	18s	G.F., O.F.	600	650
Bunn Spec.	23J	16s	163Elinvar O.F.	475	525
Bunn Spec.	26J	18s	O.F.	6500	7500
Bridge Models, semi-common					
	15J	12s	G.F., O.F.	55	75
	17J	12s	G.F., O.F.	45	60
	21J	12s	G.F., O.F.	110	135
	23J	12s	G.F., O.F.	165	195
Abe Lincoln, semi-common					
	21J	12s	G.F., O.F.	145	175
Bridge, semi-common					
	15J	16s	G.F., O.F.	55	75
	17J	16s	G.F., O.F.	85	105
	19J	16s	G.F., O.F.	165	195
	21J	16s	G.F., O.F.	175	210
	23J	16s	G.F., O.F.	325	365
Keywinds:					
American - S.	7J	18s	O.F.	95	115
Arlington - S.	7J	8s	H.	165	195
Bates - S.	7J	18s	O.F.	145	175
Bunn - S.	15J	18s	O.F.	195	235
Currier - S.	11J	18s	O.F.	235	265
Columbia - S.	7J	18s	O.F.	145	175
Dean - S.	7J	18s	O.F.	145	175
Hoyte - S.	9J	18s	O.F.	145	175
Miller - S.	15J	18s	O.F.	145	175
Mason - S.	7J	18s	O.F.	145	175
Stuart - S.	15J	18s	O.F.	145	175

The Railroads

Pictures of a Steam Locomotive on Plates.

				Buy	Sell
S	11J	18s	O.F.	$ 200	$ 245

First Model, 1/2 plates, see picture section

				Buy	Sell
	16J	16s	G.F., H.	185	210
	15J	16s	G.F., H.	155	175
	11J	16s	G.F., H.	135	160
	16J	6s	G.F., H.	175	195
	11J	6s	G.F., H.	145	175
	7J	6s	G.F., H.	85	125

Maden Lane Model

				Buy	Sell
	17J	18s	G.F., H.	245	295

Ladies' Types:

				Buy	Sell
	7J	0s	G.F., H.	115	155
	15J	0s	G.F., H.	155	200
	7J	6s	G.F., H.	115	145
	11J	6s	G.F., H.	125	160
	15J	6s	G.F., H.	165	200
	7J	8s	G.F., H.	135	175
	11J	8s	G.F., H.	150	195
	15J	8s	G.F., H.	185	225

Multi-Color

				Buy	Sell
	14K, 17J	18s	H.	1900	2100
	18K, 17J	18s	H.	2100	2300

Box Cases

				Buy	Sell
	14K, 17J	18s	H.	1450	1550
	18K, 17J	18s	H.	1750	1900
	14K, 17J	16s	H.	800	900

Multi-Color
Box Cases

				Buy	Sell
	14K, 17J	16s	H.	1200	1300
	14K, 17J	12s	H.	950	1100
	14K, 15J	6s	H.	850	950

Fancy dial add 10% to above prices.

Illinois made many watches with names of towns and cities after their own state. You will see some of these are also railroads. If you come across any you can evaluate them by increasing the price by 50% over the bridge model prices.

Sterling
Forest City
Sangamo
Columbia
Lakeside

Texas Special
Hudson
Santa Fe Special
Eureka
Ill. Central

Wolverine	Ambassador
The Master	Railway Special
The King	Miller
The Queen	Rockland
Lakeshore	Chieftain
Elite	Rock Island
The Leader	Diamond
Geo. Washington	Diamond Palace
Penn. Special	Timelock
Grant	Time King
Cres	Ill. Winner
Stuart	Superior

Benjamin Franklin Models

			Buy	Sell
26J	18s	O.F.	$3000	$3400
19J	18s	G.F., O.F.	275	325
21J	18s	G.F., O.F.	250	300
23J	18s	G.F., O.F.	450	550
24J	18s	G.F., O.F.	950	1050
25J	18s	G.F., O.F.	2000	2200

If the above is 16 size use same price.

Washington Co. Made by Illinois

Scarce Lafayette

				Buy	Sell
	24J	18s	O.F.	1000	1100
Liberty Bell	17J	16s	G.F., O.F.	165	185
	17J	18s	G.F., O.F.	145	185
Senate	17J	16s	G.F., O.F.	165	185
Potomac	17J	18s	G.F., O.F.	145	185
Army-Navy	19J	18s	G.F., O.F.	225	245
	17J	18s	G.F., O.F.	195	225

Hunting case 20% increase, mint 40% increase.

Burlington Watch Co.,

Made by Illinois under Burlington Watch Co.
Also made by Elgin, Scarce

				Buy	Sell
Burlington	19J		O.F.	125	165
Burlington Sp.	21J	16s	H.	175	220
Elgin Burlington	17J		O.F.	110	135
Burlington Bulldog					
	17J	16s	O.F.	125	145

Mint 50% increase. Hunting add 50%.

Iowa Watch Co.

Made by Illinois

				Buy	Sell
Lincoln	15J	18s	O.F.	175	225

Keystone Standard Watch Co., Lancaster, Pa. 1886
Purchased the factory of the Lancaster Watch Co. at
Lancaster, Pa.

			Buy	Sell
	6s	G.F., H.	$ 115	$ 155
Semi-scarce	16s	G.F., O.F.	100	135

Hunting case increase 40%
Dust cover 60% increase, mint 50% increase.

Knickerbocker Watch Co., New York, N.Y. 1890-1930
Made lower grade watches to compete for the dollar watch
market.

Semi-scarce	12s	G.F., O.F.	$ 60	$ 90

Lancaster Watch Co., Lancaster, Pa. 1877-1886
Successor to the Adams & Perry Watch Mfg . Co. Well Known
models were:
Keystone
Lancaster
Elderson
Keystone Standard
Melrose
Franklin
Record
West End
New Era
In 1886 the company was sold to the Keystone Standard Watch
Co.

Scarce	17J	16s	H., G.F.	$ 125	$ 175
	7J	18s	O.F.	110	145
	17J	16s	O.F.	165	210

West End model keywind

	16s	H., G.F.	300	365

The Independent Watch Co., Fredonia, N.Y. 1880-1883
Watches were supplied by several American Companies. Dial
and movements were inscribed "Independent Watch Co."
They had difficulty in marketing their product and they
reorganized in 1883 as the Fredonia Watch Co.

Rare		$ 525	$ 600

**Ingersoll, Robert H., & Bros., Waterbury, Conn., Trenton,
N.J., and New York, N.Y. 1892-1922**
Contracted to make the Waterbury Watch under their own
name. Later produced watches in Waterbury and Trenton. By
1919 50,000,000 had been sold. Their advertising slogan was

"The watch that made the dollar famous". The first model was called "Universal" scores followed.
Common to very desirable. Made mostly inexpensive dollar watches.

			Buy	Sell
			$ 10	$ 15
Regular watches	16s		40	60
17J	16s	G.F., O.F.	95	135
19J	16s	G.F., O.F.	125	175
21J	16s	G.F., O.F.	150	210

International Watch Co., Jersey City, N.J. about 1905

This company made an inexpensive nickel plated watch to compete with Ingersoll. The company lasted only a short time.

$ 25 $ 35

Kankakee Watch Co., Kankakee, Illinois about 1901

Probably became the McIntyre Watch Co. Little is known about either company.
Rare

$3500 $4000

Above E. F. or better condition.

Manhattan Watch Co., New York, N.Y. 1883-1891

Made and cased 18 size movements, both open face and hunting. Thousands were produced all stem wind and stem set.
Semi-scarce 18s $ 175 $ 225
Hunting case 20% increase.

Montgomery Ward

Common to scarce-made by Seth Thomas.

			Buy	Sell
17J	18s	G.F., H.	$ 245	$ 295
17J	18s	G.F., O.F.	145	185

Manistee Watch Co., Manistee, Mich. about 1900

Made lower quality watches for a competitive market.

				Buy	Sell
Rare	16s	G.F., H.	$ 375	$ 425
15J	18s	G.F., O.F.	225	275

Marion Watch Co., Jersey City, N.J. 1873-1875

Formerly the United States Watch Co. of Marion, N.J. They were only in business a short time before they went into bankruptcy. The machinery was sold to various companies among them the Fredonia Watch Co., Fitchburg Watch Co., and the Bowman Watch Co.
Rare   All Sizes $ 450 $ 500
Above E.F. or better condition.

New Haven Watch Co., New Haven, Conn. 1883-1887
Made a low price watch. About 1885 the factory was moved to
New Jersey and became the Trenton Watch Co.

	Buy	Sell
Inexpensive Dollar Watch	$ 25	$ 40

New York Chronograph Watch Co., N.Y., N.Y. about 1883
Produced in the Manhattan Watch Co. factory. Name was put
on the watch at the request of the jobber.
Rare

New York Standard Watch Co., Jersey City, N.J. 1885-1925
This company was very successful during its long history.
Among the models were:
Crown
Dan Patch
Columbia
New Era
Excelsior
Regent
Wilmington
Higrade
Ideal
A very desirable model is one with a *Worm Gear* visible thru the
cut out star on the plate.

		Buy	Sell
Common	16s-18s O.F.	$ 25	$ 35

Hunting case increase 40%, mint 100%.

New York Standard Watch Co.

				Buy	Sell
Worm Gear Models				$ 345	$ 400

Names that might appear on watches made by Standard.

				Buy	Sell
Columbus	7J		G.F., H.	55	75
Crown	7J		G.F., O.F.	30	50
Excelsior	7J		G.F., O.F.	30	50
New Era	7J		G.F., O.F.	35	60
Perfection	7J-15J		G.F., H.	35	60
Ladies' types:	7J	6s	G.F., H.	75	105
	7J	6s	G.F., O.F.	25	40
Regular Type Nickel					
	15J	18s	O.F.	45	55
Rice Nickel	15J	18s	O.F.	65	85

New York Watch Co., Springfield, Mass. 1867-1876
Formerly the Mozart Watch Co., Providence, Rhode Island. The
company was doing good until the panic of 1873. Then they
struggled along until 1875, and rather than close the doors,

they added new capital. They managed to get reorganized under the name New York Watch Manufacturing Co. After 8 months this reorganization proved a failure and again was reorganized as the Hampden Watch Co. First movements were produced in the 1867-1876 period by the New York Watch Co.:

Keywind models:

				Buy	Sell
Springfield	15J	18s	O.F.	$ 175	$ 200
Homer Foot	15J	18s	O.F.	300	350
J.A. Briggs	15J	18s	O.F.	300	350
John L. King	15J	18s	O.F.	225	250
No. 5	15J	18s	O.F.	150	200
H.G. Norton	15J	18s	O.F.	225	275
Albert Clark	15J	18s	O.F.	300	355
T.E. Studley	15J	18s	H.	275	325
John Hancock	15J	18s	H.	285	335
Rice	15J	18s	O.F.	250	275
Railway	15J	18s	O.F.	250	285

7J models $50 less above prices.

Stem winds:

			Buy	Sell
E.W. Bond	18s	N., O.F.	95	125
State St.	18s	N., O.F.	95	125
Perry	18s	N., O.F.	95	125

Hunting add 50% more to above prices.

McIntyre Watch Co., Melrose, Mass. About 1905
Probably purchased the factory of the Kankakee Watch Company. Not much is known about either.

Melrose Watch Co., Melrose, Mass. 1866-1868
Formerly the Tremont Watch Company. Moved from Boston, forced to close its doors because of shortage of working capital. Machinery sold in England to the England Watch Company. About 2500 watches were made.

				Buy	Sell
Semi-rare	15J	18s	N., O.F.	$ 650	$850

Mozart Watch Co., Ann Arbor, Mich. 1868-1871
Don J. Mozart (1820-1877) was an extremely gifted watchmaker. He was working on an unusual 17 size three wheel movement with a chronograph lever escapement, when in 1866 he interested a group of investors in Springfield, Mass., to build a factory to produce his watch. The company was called the New York Watch Company. The model movement was very disappointing and Mr. Mozart left the company after a year. He kept on working to perfect his unusual movement and he

relocated in Ann Arbor, Michigan. He now thought he had his movement perfected and he managed to get a new start in Ann Arbor. For some reason not one watch was completed, though hundreds of parts were made. In 1870, the company ran out of funds and closed. Mozart did eventually assemble and case 10 watches. These watches were presented to stockholders. The machinery was finally sold in 1871 to the Rock Island Watch Company of Rock Island, Illinois.

Nashua Watch Company, Nashua, New Hampshire 1859-1862
This company made about 1000 movements. They were never placed on the market due to financial difficulties. Factory and movements were sold to the American Watch Company of Waltham. New top plates were made for the movements and they were inscribed "Appleton, Tracy & Company".

New Jersey Watch Co., Newark, N.J.
Red Jacket Model   7J   18s

Newark Watch Company, Newark, N.J. 1863-1870
This was a very successful company in the two years in business. They increased production from 400-1500 movements. Sold to Cornell Watch Company in 1870.

				Buy	Sell
Keywind	15J	18s	N, O.F.	$ 475	$ 550

Non-Magnet Watch Co. of America, N.Y. and Chicago

Non-Magnetic Watch Co., Chicago, Ill. 1884
Move from New York, N.Y.

				Buy	Sell
Non-Magnetic Chronograph		H.		$ 650	$ 700
Non-Magnetic Repeaters		H.		3200	3500
Non-Magnetic Watch	7J-17J		O.F.	100	145
Illinois Models	17J	18s	O.F.	125	165
	17J	16s	H.	175	220
	17J	16s	O.F.	100	145
Swiss Models		16s	O.F.	75	100

New England Watch Co., Waterbury, Conn. 1898-1914
Formerly Waterbury Watch Company. They made a watch with Duplex escapement. The skeletonized gilt movement models are conversation pieces. In 1914 the company was sold to R.H. Ingersoll & Bros.

				Buy	Sell
Very desirable	16s-14s	O.F.		$ 65	$ 85
Duplex Escapements				65	90

			Buy	Sell
Chronograph, Dan Patch		G.F.	$ 225	$ 275
21J	16s	O.F.	165	225
Addison Model	6s	O.F.	60	85

Otay Watch Company, Otay, Calif. 1889-1890

This company built their own machinery and plant to manufacture watches. They lasted one year. The movement was similar to Columbus Watch company movements. The factory was closed in 1890. The following models were made:

- P. H. Wheeler
- Native Son
- R. D. Perry
- Golden Gate
- F. A. Kimball
- Overland Mail

Only six models of the Overland Mail were made. This model was publicized as "The Official Railroad Watch of Mexico". The company machinery was purchased by the Japanese Watch Company of Osaka, Japan, and moved there in 1894.

	18s	O.F., G.F.	$2650	$3000
	18s	H., G.F.	2750	3000

Philadelphia Watch Co., Philadelphia, Pa. 1886

Scarce	18s	O.F.	$ 400	$ 450
	0s-6s	H.	225	285

Pitkin, H. & J.F., East Hartford, Conn., and New York City 1838-1844

The brothers Henry and James F. Pitkin were the first to produce, by machine, watches with interchangeable parts. They produced about 800 watches. The first 50 watches were signed "H. & J.F. Pitkin". In 1841 they moved their plant to New York City. The New York watches were signed "Pitkin & Co." and some were marked "Pitkin American Lever Watch". Henry went insane and died on the way to the hospital. James started a watch case business.

Potter Watch Co., New York, N.Y. 1855-1861

William C. Potter was considered to be the finest watchmaker in America. He made about 35 top quality watch movements on special order. His brother entered the partnership and they moved their machinery to Chicago. This firm was then called

Potter Bros. Efforts were made to make excellent chronographs.

Rock Island Watch Co., Rock Island, Illinois 1871-1874
Purchased machinery from the Mozart Watch Co. No movements were marketed. Company was sold to Freeport Watch Co., Freeport, Illinois.

Reliance Watch Co., Chicago, Ill.
Made by Trenton Watch Company.

			Buy	Sell
7J	16s	O.F.	$ 40	$ 55
7J	16s	H.	65	80

George P. Reed Watch Co., Boston, Mass.

	15J	18s	$10,000	$11,000
Chronometer	15J	18s	15,000	16,000

Palmer Watch Company, Waltham, Mass. about 1870
Very little is known about this firm.

Peoria Watch Co., Peoria, Illinois 1885-1890
Company specialized in 18 size, 15 jewel, quick train railroad watches. Machinery was owned formerly by the Fredonia Watch Company of Fredonia, New York.

Non-Magnetic model		18s	G.F., H.	$ 295	$ 350
Railroad models	15J	18s	H.	300	375
		6s	H.	190	230
Keywind	17J	18s	O.F.	200	240

For serial numbers to 25,000 add 20%.

Railroad Watch Co., Cleveland, Ohio, See Ball Watch Co.

Rockford Watch Company, Rockford, Ill. 1873-1915
This was a very successful company, greatly favored by the railroads. Their factory was completed in 1876, with their first watch being made the same year. Many employees had come to Rockford from the Cornell Watch Company.
Common Type Rockfords:

17J	12s	G.F., O.F.	$ 35	$ 50
15J	16s	G.F., O.F.	65	90
17J	16s	G.F., H.	155	195
17J	18s	G.F., O.F.	95	130
17J	18s	G.F., H.	145	220

Railroad Grades:				Buy	Sell
Up & Down Indicators	21J	16s	G.F., O.F.	$ 695	$ 750
	23J	16s	G.F., O.F.	775	825
	23J	18s	G.F., O.F.	950	1050
Number 900	24J	18s	G.F., O.F.	1550	1650
Number 800	24J	18s	G.F., H.	1550	1650
	25J	18s	G.F., O.F.	2000	2100
	26J	18s	G.F., O.F.	3500	4000
Full Plate:					
	24J	18s	G.F., O.F.	1550	1650
	21J	18s	G.F., O.F.	165	200
	21J	16s	G.F., O.F.	160	200
Bridge Models:					
	21J	16s	G.F., O.F.	235	265
	23J	16s	G.F., O.F.	400	450
Winnebago Models:					
	17J	18s	G.F., O.F.	165	195
	21J	16s	G.F., O.F.	210	250
	19J	16s	G.F., O.F.	350	400
	17J	16s	G.F., O.F.	155	195
Dome Models - Nickel Plates:					
	15J	17s	G.F., O.F.	135	165
	15J	17s	G.F., H.	225	265
	11J	17s	G.F., O.F.	175	220
Dome Models - Brass Plates:					
	9J	17s	G.F., O.F.	100	145
Ladies' sizes in Dome Models:					
	15J		G.F., H.	250	325
Ladies' Regular Type:					
	15J	6s	G.F., H.	265	300
	7J	6s	G.F., H.	175	210
	15J	0s	G.F., H.	225	275
	7J	0s	G.F., H.	145	185
Scarce 8s Ladies	15J		G.F., H.	300	375
Pocahontas Model:					
	17J	16s	G.F., O.F.	200	250
	17J	12s	G.F., O.F.	145	190
Iroquois:					
	17J	16s	G.F., O.F.	195	245
	17J	12s	G.F., O.F.	145	175
	15J	0s	G.F., H.	175	210
Winona:	15J	0s	G.F., H.	195	225

Fancy dial add 50% to above prices.

Plymouth Watch Co., made by Rockford for Sears & Roebuck Co.

				Buy	Sell
King Edward	21J	18s	G.F., O.F.	$ 300	$ 350
Prince of Wales	21J	16s	G.F., O.F.	200	245
Plymouth	15J	0s	G.F., H.	175	225

Sears, Roebuck & Co., Chicago, Ill. about 1884

Watches were made by the Illinois Watch Company and sold through the mail.

Sears and Roebuck Watch Co., Chicago, Ill. 1900-1920

				Buy	Sell
Elgin Models	17J	16s	H.	$ 195	$ 210

Illinois models of Sears are scarce

Swiss models		16s	H.	115	130
Ill. and Elgin	17J	18s		225	255

The Self-Winding Watch Co., Chicago, Ill. about 1884

This was a very fine handmade watch constructed by a German immigrant. He made about 35 watches. They sold extremely well. They were 18 size, lever escapement and fully jeweled. The winding mechanism was of the gravity type. The motion of the body moves a heavy steel crescent which is connected to the rachet on the winding arbor.

Rare	Gravity type	18s	winding	$3400	$3700

Seth Thomas Watch Co., Thomaston, Conn. 1883-1915

This was a division of the Seth Thomas Clock Company, which was established in 1814. Thousands of watches were made and sold. They made a popular seller in various sizes, grades, and jewel content. The company quit making watches in 1915.

Semi-scarce	7J-17J	all sizes	O.F.	$ 95	$ 125
	21J	18s	O.F.	155	200
Maiden Lane	25J		H.	2750	2900
Maiden Lane	21J		H.	375	425
	14K, 28J	18s	O.F.	4000	4500
Multi-Color:					
	14K, 15J	18s	H.	2250	2500
	14K, 15J	16s	H.	1250	1450
	14K, 15J	12s	H.	850	950
	14K, 15J	6s	H.	850	950
Ladies' Type:					
	7J	6s	G.F., H.	135	160
	15J	6s	G.F., H.	185	210
	7J	0s	G.F., H.	145	175
	15J	0s	G.F., H.	175	210

Maiden Lane Models:

			Buy	Sell
21J	18s	G.F., O.F.	$ 245	$ 295
23J	18s	G.F., O.F.	325	375
25J	18s	G.F., O.F.	3000	3250
26J	18s	G.F., O.F.	4250	4500
27J	18s	G.F., O.F.	4750	5250
21J	16s	G.F., O.F.	175	225
23J	16s	G.F., O.F.	325	375

Common Models:

			Buy	Sell
7J	18s	G.F., O.F.	65	95
7J	16s	G.F., H.	135	175
7J	12s	G.F., H.	85	120
7J	6s	G.F., H.	125	165
15J-17J	18s	G.F., O.F.	85	120
17J	16s	G.F., O.F.	65	95
17J	12s	G.F., O.F.	50	75

Fancy dial add 40% to the above prices.

Edgemere Watch Company
Made by Seth Thomas, sold by Sears Roebuck Company.

	6s-18s		$ 110	$ 145

Hunting case 25% increase, mint 50% more.

Keywinds	18s	O.F.	295	345

Wyoming Watch Company
Made by Seth Thomas

7J	18s	O.F.	$ 125	$ 145

Shell Watch Company, 1939
Made in Switzerland on special order by the Girard-Perregaux Company for the Shell Oil Company. 30,000 were ordered promoting the sale of Golden Shell Oil. The watch was skeletonized and transparent on both front and back. The watch was a 7 jewel movement.
Made for Shell Oil Co.

7J	12s	O.F.	$ 175	$ 225

South Bend Watch Co., South Bend, Ind. 1902-1933
Bought out Columbus Watch Company. Serial numbers start at 300,000.
Railroad Models

The Studebaker:	21J	18s	G.F., O.F.	$ 325	$ 375
	21J	16s	G.F., O.F.	210	250

				Buy	Sell
	21J	18s	G.F., O.F.	$ 245	$ 295
	21J	16s	G.F., O.F.	195	235
#227	21J	16s	G.F., O.F.	195	235
Polaris Model	21J, 14K	16s	O.F.	395	450

Common Models:

	19J	16s	G.F., O.F.	100	125
	19J	12s	G.F., OF.	65	95
	17J	18s	G.F., O.F.	85	105
	17J	16s	G.F., O.F.	65	85
	15J or 17J	12s	G.F., O.F.	45	65
	15J	18s	G.F., O.F.	85	110

Add 50% to the above for Hunting models.

Ladies' Type:	7J	6s	G.F., H.	$ 125	$ 155
Ladies' Model:	17J	6s	G.F., H.	200	245
	7J to 15J	6s	G.F., O.F.	55	85

Above with fancy dials add 50% to the price.

12s with Pearl Back and Bezel:

	19J	12s	O.F.	450	500

12s Chesterfield model:

	17J		G.F., O.F.		

Stevens, J. P., Watch Co., Atlanta, Georgia 1882-1887

Mr. J. P. Stevens purchased the machinery from the Bowman Company of Lancaster, Pa. The company failed after the death of the principal backer, J. C. Freeman.

				Buy	Sell
Rare up to 500 serial number original				$2000	$2200
Aurora-model	17J	18s		500	550
Elgin model	17J	18s		475	525
Illinois model	17J	18s		525	575
Waltham model	17J	18s		525	575
Hamilton model	17J	18s		625	675
Hampden model	17J	18s		625	675
Ladies	14K, 15J	6s	H.	600	650

Suffolk Watch Co., New York, and Boston about 1901

Movements made by the U.S. Watch Company.

	18s	G.F., O.F.	$ 90	$ 110

Sun Dial Watch Company, Elgin, Ill. about 1898

Made and produced by the Elgin Watch Company for the purpose of competing in the dollar watch market.

		$ 25	$ 35

Tremont Watch Co., Boston, Mass. 1864-1866

Organized by Aaron L. Dennison with plates, barrels and some minor parts made in Zurich, under Mr. Dennison's supervision. The company moved to Melrose, Mass., in 1866. There it was renamed the Melrose Watch Company.

			Buy	Sell
Semi-scarce	18s		$ 400	$ 475

Trenton Watch Co., Trenton, N.J. 1885-1908

At one time during the history of this very successful watch, the company turned out as many as 500 watches a day. R. H. Ingersoll and Bros. bought the company for production of the dollar watch.

Comm.

			Buy	Sell
Semi-scarce	7J-15J		$ 75	$ 95
	17J		125	165
Stop Watch	16s		85	110

Union Watch Co., Fitchburg, Mass.

15J	KW, KS
17J	KW, KS

U.S. Watch Company, Waltham, Mass. 1884-1888

This company was in existence about 4 years and made about 18,000 watches, all stemwind.

				Buy	Sell
The President:		18s	G.F., O.F.	$ 250	$ 295
Dome Model	7J	14s	S., O.F.	175	225
	15J or 17J	18s	G.F., O.F.	75	95
	15J or 17J	16s	G.F., O.F.	75	95
	15J or 17J	12s	G.F., O.F.	45	65
	7J	16s or 18s	G.F., O.F.	45	65
	7J	6s	G.F., H.	95	125

U.S. Watch Co., New York, N.Y. made by the U.S. Watch Co. of Waltham, Mass.

				Buy	Sell
Scarce	15J	16s	G.F., H.	$ 150	$ 175
	7J	16s	G.F., O.F.	75	90

Above E.F. or better condition.

United States Watch Co., Marion, N.J. 1864-1873

Not to be confused with the watch company in Waltham, Mass. Some of the early models were:

1867 - Frederick Atherton	1869 - John Lewis
1868 - Edwin Rollo	1870 - G. A. Reid
1869 - S. M. Beard	1870 - J. W. Dwacon
1869 - A. H. Wallace	1870 - Charles G. Knapp

The business was reorganized in 1873 and renamed the Marion Watch Company.

				Buy	Sell
Rare early Keywinds				$ 450	$ 500

Names on movements 30% increase.

Waltham Watch Co., Waltham, Mass. 1857-1957

Common to rare

Early Keywind Serial No. to 10,000				$ 245	$ 295

Names on movements 40% increase.

Keywinds 10,000 to 50,000				135	175

Mint hunting watches add 100%.

5 Minute Repeater 14K			H.	3000	3400
Model 1872	18K	16s	H.	750	850

Model 1884-1888-1892

	14K	16s	H.	550	650

Chronograph or Stop Watch

		16s	G.F.	325	375

1859, Early chronograph in Keywind Appleton Tracy Model:

	14J	18s	S., H.	500	575

Crescent St. Keywind in Railroad model:

Gold Balance	15J	18s	O.F.	250	295

Waltham Crystal Watch Plates made of Crystal:

		16s	O.F.	1950	2100

Up and Down Indicators:

Vanguard Model	23J	16s	O.F.	395	450
	21J	16s	O.F.	395	450

Premier Maximus

All diamond cap jewels	23J	16s	O.F.	2450	2650

Canadian Railway Time Service

	17J	18s	G.F., O.F.	275	325

Dominion Railway

	17J	18s	G.F., O.F.	275	325

Railway Time Keeper

Rare	15J	18s			

Rarity		Size	Mintage	Buy	Sell
Maximus (Opera)	17J	0/16s		$1200	$1300
Maximum (Ligne)	17J	16s		750	850
Maximus	14K, 19J	16s	11840	495	550
Maximum	14K, 21J	16s	6900	550	600
Maximus	14K, 23J	16s	17012	650	750
Maximum (L)	14K, 17J		500	1200	1300
Premier Maximus	14K, 23J		1100	2450	2650
Colonial Maximus	14K, 21J		200		
Colonial Maximus	14K, 23J		2000	850	1000
Colonial A Maximus	14K, 21J		1100	950	1050
Penn. Special	14K, 21J		53		
Riverside	7J	16s	11341	75	85
Riverside	15J	16s	77560	100	110
Riverside	16J	16s	3050	175	195
Riverside	17J	16s	91095	75	95
Riverside	18J	16s			
Riverside	19J	16s	126749	135	175
Riverside	21J	16s	15700	145	165
Crescent St.	15J	8s	48100	85	95
Crescent St.	17J	18s	8400	155	165
Crescent St.	19J	18s	11285	135	175
Crescent St.	21J	16s	163865	135	165
Vanguard	17J	16s	3000	325	350
Vanguard	19J	16s	16450	135	175
Vanguard	21J	16s	51706	200	250
Vanguard	23J	16s	236371	165	200
645	19J	16s	G.F.	135	175
645	21J	16s	G.F.	145	185
845	21J	18s	G.F.	245	295
Canadian Pacific	17J	18s		245	295
Santa Fe Route	17J	18s		75	95
P.S. Bartlett	15J			95	120
P.S. Bartlett	17J			125	165
P.S. Bartlett gilded plates		18s		75	95
P.S. Bartlett Keywind		18s			

All the watches on this page are O.F. type and G.F.
Prices same for 16s or 18s.

				Buy	Sell
Appleton Tracy	15J		O.F.	$ 115	$ 140
Appleton Tracy	17J		O.F.	120	155
Appleton Tracy Keywind			O.F.	75	105

Above 16s or 18s same price.
Hunting cases 20% increase.
Semi-common Walthams:

				Buy	Sell
Broadway	7J-17J		S., O.F.	75	95
Hillside	7J-17J		S., O.F.	75	95
Wm. Ellery	7J		G.F., O.F.	75	95
Wm. Ellery	11J-17J		G.F., O.F.	75	100
Ladies' Type:		0s-6s	G.F., H.	145	175
		0s-6s	G.F., O.F.	35	60
Royal	17J	16s	G.F., O.F.	100	145
Royal	21J	16s	G.F., O.F.	145	185
Ensign	7J	16s	S., O.F.	65	90

Above in hunting cases add 25%.

				Buy	Sell
Bond St.	7J	14s	S., O.F.	65	85
Bond St. Rare pin set			O.F.	125	175

The following are Waltham's very special grade of Gentlemen's watches.

				Buy	Sell
Verithin	14K, 17J	12s	O.F.	200	245
Opera Watch	17J	12s	O.F.	200	235

Special Models:

				Buy	Sell
Model 72	15J	16s	G.F., H.	300	365
Model 84 & 88	15J	16s	G.F., H.	185	235
Model 92	15J	16s	G.F., H.	175	225

Colonial Series:

				Buy	Sell
	17J	12s	G.F., O.F.	65	90
	17J	16s	G.F., O.F.	100	135
	14K, 19J		O.F.	255	295
Colonial A	14K, 21J		O.F.	255	295
Colonial Royal:	17J	16s	G.F., O.F.	75	100

Opera Watch with diamond set in platinum

				Buy	Sell
	17J	12s	O.F.	1000	1100
18s Waltham hunting case in 14K				750	850
18s Waltham Watch in 18K hunting				850	950
16s Waltham in 14K hunting case				450	550
Multi-color gold	14K	18s	H.	2250	2450

Multi-Color Gold:

				Buy	Sell
		16s	H.	1300	1400
		12s	H.	900	1000
		6s	H.	850	950

Multi-Color box case:

				Buy	Sell
	14K	18s	H.	2650	2750

			Buy	Sell
14K	16s	H.	$1600	$1700

Fancy dials add 50% to the above prices.

Any Waltham watch in mint hunting cases add 100% to the book price. Waltham made millions of common 7J and 15J watches from 12s to 18s of G.F. $ 45 $ 90

Waltham-Howard Company, 1910

There were some Howards made at Waltham. Some have Waltham dials but the movements are Howard. These are very scarce.

21J	16s	G.F., H.	$ 350	$ 400
14K, 21J	12s	O.F.	375	425

Wm. Ellery, Boston, Mass. 1857

These watches were made in Boston before they moved to Waltham and changed their name to the American Watch Co., then to the Waltham Watch Company. These are the first Waltham watches and are scarce, but can be found.

Keywinds Silver	16s	H.	$ 225	$ 275

Warren Manufacturing Company, Roxbury, Mass. 1853

Only five known today of one hundred made. (See Howard, Davis & Dennison).

Witchita Watch Co., 1887

Very rare. They made about 5 watches.

Waterbury Watch Co., Waterbury, Conn. 1880-1898

This company was organized to fill the need to market a watch selling for under $5.00. Mr. D. Buck of Worchester, Mass.,was an excellent watchmaker. He was engaged by the company to design this watch. He submitted a novel design called the "Rotary Movement". The movement revolved in the case one complete turn every hour, and carried a minute hand with it. It was a duplex escapement with a 9 foot mainspring. There were only 58 interchangeable parts in the movement. The first were made by Benedict & Burnham who turned out 100 movements a day. The watch became a give-away item for commercial products, such as suits of clothes and winning games of chance. This down graded the value of the watch and the sales dropped. The company failed in 1898. It was reorganized with fresh capital as the New England Watch Co.

Common			$ 45	$ 65
Scarce Rotary			115	135
Columbian	6s	H.	110	135
American General 15J	16s	O.F.	65	95

Ball Watch Co., Cleveland, Ohio about 1900

Webb C. Ball was the watchmaker. Ball watch parts were ordered through Waltham, Hamilton, Elgin, Ill., and Switzerland. He damasked swirls into the back plate of the movements. Some of his first watches were marked Railroad Watch Co., Cleveland, these are rare.

Waltham Official R.R.

				Buy	Sell
	15J	16s	O.F.	$ 95	$ 120
	17J	16s	O.F.	95	120
	21J	16s	O.F.	225	265
Howard Ball	17J	17s	O.F.	850	950
Hampden	17J	18s	O.F.	295	350
Commercial Standard:					
	15J	18s	O.F.	145	175
	17J	16s	O.F.	105	135
Illinois Official Standard:					
	17J	16s	O.F.	150	185
	21J	16s	O.F.	225	275
Sangamo	23J	16s	O.F.	375	425
Railroad Watch Co.					
Rare	17J	18s	O.F.	2750	3000
Hamilton Official Standard:					
#999	17J	18s	O.F.	195	225
#999	21J	18s	O.F.	295	345
#999	23J	18s	O.F.	425	475
#999	19J	18s	O.F.	275	325
#998B	23J	16s	O.F. 6-Pos.	525	575
#999B	21J	16s	O.F. 6-Pos.	325	375

Hunting cases add 20%.

Ladies' type in any make:

		Buy	Sell
0s-6s	G.F., H.	210	235
0s-6s	G.F., O.F.	65	95

Must be E.F. condition, mint add 50%.

Switzerland type Balls are scarce and should be in your collection.

		Buy	Sell
7-17J	12s to 16s	$ 95	$ 120
Ball R.R. Traimater Wrist Watch		$ 145	$ 175

Webb C. Ball, Howard Model, 1886

	Buy	Sell
Rare	6000	6500

Washington Watch Co., (see Ill. Watch Co.)
Washington Watch Co., Washington, D.C. about 1872.

Made 40 or 50 watches and lasted about a year. Most of the material was purchased by the Illinois Watch Company.

Gruen Watch Co., Cincinnati, Ohio (assembled)
Swiss made, Semi scarce.
50th Anniversary Model. Solid Gold movement:

				Buy	Sell
500 made	23J	12s	O.F.	$4000	$4500
Dresden Models:	21J	18s	G.F., O.F.	450	525
	21J	16s	G.F., H.	300	350
Common Models-Verithin:					
	21J	12s	G.F., O.F.	75	100
	19J	12s	G.F., O.F.	55	75
	17J	12s	G.F., O.F.	45	65
Gruen Guild:					
	17J	12s	G.F., O.F.	85	105
Chronometer Balance Models:					
	14K, 21J	12s	O.F.	195	225
Up and Down Indicators:					
	14K, 23J	16s	O.F.	1350	1450
18K Repeater 1 Minute:					
	32J	16s	O.F.	5000	5500

-See Gruen Article

PRICES ON WATCHES AT TIME OF PRODUCTION

The following is a list of prices that watch movements sold for around 1900.

Rockford	16J	O.F.	30Hamilton	17J	5P.O.F.	
N.Y. Standard	7J	New Era			$	4
Illinois	21J	16s				65
Waltham Vanguard	21J	16s				56
Seth Thomas	21J	Maiden Lane				50
Hampden John Hancock	21J					33
South Bend	21J	16s				35
U.S. Watch Co. †	17J					68
Columbus	21J Time King					25
Howard	17J	16s				75
Waltham	7J	18s				8

†U.S. Watch Co., Waltham, Mass.

DATE OF PRODUCTION

Columbus Watch Co.

Serial No.	Year		Serial No.	Year
20,000	1883			
90,000	1884		194,000	1894
125,000	1885		199,000	1895
135,000	1886		202,000	1896
147,000	1887		210,000	1897
155,000	1888		217,000	1898
165,000	1889		221,000	1899
175,000	1890		226,000	1900
181,000	1891		245,000	1901
185,000	1892		266,000	1902
188,000	1893		289,000	1903

South Bend starts at 300,000.

Elgin

Serial No.	Year		Serial No.	Year
1-100	1864,65,66		3,550,000	1889
100	1867		4,000,000	1890
31,000	1868		4,400,000	1891
71,000	1869		4,890,000	1892
101,000	1870		5,000,000	1893
126,000	1871		5,500,000	1894
152,000	1872		6,000,000	1895
176,000	1873		6,550,000	1896
210,000	1874		7,000,000	1897
310,000	1875		7,550,000	1898
410,ooo	1876		8,100,000	1899
510,000	1877		9,100,000	1900
552,000	1878		9,350,000	1901
601,000	1879		9,755,000	1902
701,000	1880		10,100,000	1903
801,000	1881		11,100,000	1904
1,000,000	1882		12,100,000	1905
1,000,000	1881		12,500,000	1906
1,440,000	1883		13,100,000	1907
1,650,000	1884		13,550,000	1908
1,850,000	1885		14,100,000	1909
2,000,000	1886		15,100,000	1910
2,550,000	1887			
3,000,000	1888			

Hamilton

1-100	1893	1,575,000	1917
1,000	1894	1,700,000	1919
5,500	1895	1,850,000	1921
6,500	1896	2,000,000	1923
9,500	1897	2,250,000	1925
16,000	1901	2,300,000	1927
340,000	1903	2,400,000	1929
420,000	1905	2,500,000	1931
750,000	1907	2,550,000	1933
1,000,000	1909	2,650,000	1935
1,250,000	1911	2,600,000	1936
1,350,000	1913	3,000,000	1940
1,455,000	1915		

Hampden Watch Co.
Springfield, Mass. and Canton, Ohio

100-20,000	1876	1,655,000	1893
20,000-50,000	1877	1,750,000	1894
150,000	1878	1,850,000	1895
200,000	1879	1,955,000	1896
360,000	1880	2,155,000	1898
365,000	1881	2,250,000	1899
475,000	1882	2,350,000	1900
577,000	1883	2,445,000	1901
690,000	1884	2,600,000	1903
850,000	1885	2,875,000	1905
950,000	1886	3,000,000	1907
1,100,000	1887	3,100,000	1909
1,150,000	1888	3,800,000	1915
1,250,000	1889	4,500,000	1922
1,350,000	1890	4,700,000	1926
1,450,000	1891		
1,550,000	1892		

Howard

1-1,000	1857	265,000	1878
2,000	1858	410,000	1884
2,600	1859	471,000	1886
31,100	1860	610,000	1890
35,000	1861	700,00	1896
45,000	1864	800,000	1900
61,000	1867	990,000	1909
71,000	1868	1,200,000	1915
101,000	1872	1,450,000	1921
221,000	1876	1,550,000	1930

Illinois Watch Co.

1-1,000	1869	845,000	1898
15,000	1871	925,000	1899
60,000	1874	1,550,000	1902
100,000	1876	2,000,000	1904
140,000	1878	2,500,000	1906
190,000	1880	3,850,000	1910
220,000	1882	4,000,000	1912
275,000	1884	4,250,000	1916
300,000	1886	4,255,000	1918
365,000	1888	4,450,000	1920
430,000	1890	4,860,000	1923
475,000	1892	5,300,000	1925
575,000	1894	5,650,000	1927
675,000	1896		

Seth Thomas Watch Co.

1-4,000	1884	501,000	1900
9,500	1886	601,000	1902
51,000	1888	700,000	1904
105,000	1890	800,00	1906
175,000	1892	1,000,000	1908
245,000	1894	1,300,000	1910
330,000	1896	2,350,000	1912
417,000	1898	3,650,000	1914

Rockford Watch Co.

1-1,000	1874	230,000	1894
1,000-7,000	1875	321,000	1896
18,500	1877	355,000	1898
41,000	1879	410,000	1900
61,000	1881	481,000	1902
81,000	1883	650,000	1907
102,000	1885	800,000	1911
127,000	1887	879,000	1913
150,000	1889	830,000	1915
175,000	1891		

Waltham

1-1,000	1850-57	5,000,000	1890
14,500	1858	6,000,000	1892
21,000	1860	7,000,000	1894
35,000	1862	8,000,000	1896
45,000	1863	10,000,000	1901
185,000	1865	13,500,000	1905
330,000	1867	15,500,000	1907
475,000	1869	18,000,000	1910
525,000	1870	21,000,000	1915
650,000	1872	23,500,000	1919
730,000	1874	25,500,000	1925
950,000	1876	27,500,000	1929
1,100,000	1878	29,500,000	1936
1,500,000	1880	31,000,000	1942
1,800,000	1882	32,500,000	1945
2,300,000	1884	33,000,000	1950
3,300,000	1886	35,500,000	1958
3,900,000	1888		

For information on how to obtain the carrying cases to hold watches and dealer trays, write for brochure.

• • • • • • • •

For extra copies send $7.95 to Criss Coin Enterprises, 125 N. Almont Ave., Imlay City, Michigan 48444.

Name ____

Street ____

City _______________________________ State ___________ Zip ________

Number of copies ____________

Dealers send for wholesale prices.

FRONT COVER
Left to right top
Digital Watch of 1897
Elgin U.S. Army Timer
Center
18 size Nielo Hunting Case, Airplane of 1907
Left to right bottom
Illinois in Nielo Hunting Case
German Nielo Watch with Bicycle

BACK COVER
Top
8 size 18K ladies' Waltham keywind
Left to right
12 size 14K Elgin
18 size 18K Howard
Center
18K enamel keywind
Bottom
14K English Fusee made in 1825
Multi-color 16 size South Bend
21 jewel 14K Hampden